"I wish that I'd had this book when I was starting my career. I also wish that I'd had the incredible networking tools available today. Joe does a remarkable job integrating them into what is a very old set of success principles."

—Randy Conrads
FOUNDER OF CLASSMATES.COM, CEO OF REDWEEK.COM

"A mesmerizing look at the power of *The Kingdom Net* to set captives free from bondage, re-bind them in missional relationships, and defrag a fragmented world."

—Leonard Sweet
BEST-SELLING AUTHOR OF *VIRAL: HOW SOCIAL NETWORKING IS POISED TO IGNITE REVIVAL* AND PROFESSOR AT DREW UNIVERSITY AND GEORGE FOX UNIVERSITY

"Relationships and the networks that connect them are the foundation of every successful business. The quality of these relational networks with customers, employees, leaders, vendors and suppliers determine success or failure. In *The Kingdom Net,* Joe Castleberry connects the time-proven networking strategy of Jesus Christ with today's society in a way that's a must-read for every business person, leader, or follower of Christ."

—Steve Gandara
CO-FOUNDER OF EXCELLENT CULTURES, INC.
WWW.EXCELLENTCULTURES.COM

"I found myself captivated and unable to stop reading and learning. This is a life-changing book that will drive people to maximize God's calling on their lives."

—**Kirsten Miller**
PRESIDENT, NORPRO, INC.

"Written by a gifted networker, this engaging book combines sound theory, exemplary models, and practical advice. Unlike many self-help books on building networks, Dr. Castleberry challenges us not to develop our skills in networking to serve our own agendas and draw people into our programs, but to practice networking for the sake of advancing God's interests in this world and drawing people into God's net."

—**David de Silva**
TRUSTEES' DISTINGUISHED PROFESSOR OF NEW TESTAMENT
AND GREEK, ASHLAND THEOLOGICAL SEMINARY

"Our horizontal relationships have vertical consequences. In *The Kingdom Net,* Joe Castleberry frames the optics for a Christ-centered, kingdom-collaborative networking apparatus that will exponentially enrich all aspects of life. Dr. Castleberry equips us with practical engagement tools poised to catapult our families, ministries, professions, and lives into new heights of effectiveness and efficiency."

—**Rev. Samuel Rodriguez**
PRESIDENT OF THE NATIONAL HISPANIC
CHRISTIAN LEADERSHIP CONFERENCE
HISPANIC EVANGELICAL ASSOCIATION

"Since we were undergraduates together back in the 1980s, I have watched Joe Castleberry grow as a leader and a man of godly integrity. Joe, as his recent book unpacks, takes the trendy concept of networking and explores its biblical roots. Collaboration for kingdom purposes is the way God has called us to lead, and this book will help show you how."

—Dr. Barry H. Corey
PRESIDENT OF BIOLA UNIVERSITY

"Joseph Castleberry has written an engaging, informative, and accessible book for laypeople and especially aspiring professionals. But scholars and theologians ought not overlook it. *The Kingdom Net* provides a kingdom-and-network christology, ecclesiology, and missiology. All anticipating the coming reign of God ought to read this book."

—Amos Yong
DEAN AND J. RODMAN WILLIAMS PROFESSOR OF THEOLOGY,
SCHOOL OF DIVINITY, REGENT UNIVERSITY

"How did we ever miss the task of doing theology of NETworks— having read this book it seems so obvious! Joe Castleberry's passionate book is not only a creative missiological-theological study but also a hands-on practical guide into the best biblical insights of how to connect with people for the sake of the kingdom. The NET value of this primer is immense!"

—Veli-Matti Kärkkäinen
PROFESSOR OF SYSTEMATIC THEOLOGY, FULLER
THEOLOGICAL SEMINARY AND DOCENT OF ECUMENICS,
UNIVERSITY OF HELSINKI, FINLAND

THE KINGDOM NET
LEARNING TO NETWORK LIKE JESUS

JOSEPH CASTLEBERRY

MY HEALTHY CHURCH
MyHealthyChurch.com

Published by My Healthy Church
1445 North Boonville Avenue
Springfield, Missouri 65802

Cover design by Cary Bates
Interior design by Prodigy Pixel (www.prodigypixel.com)

ISBN: 978-1-62423-081-3
Printed in the United States of America
16 15 14 13 • 1 2 3 4 5

To the Reverend Jesse Ollie Owens,
whom I met as a Youth Camper in 1974
and from whom I began to learn the value
of building friendships with the people I admire.

and to Sam, may God
use you to fish for
people!

CONTENTS

FOREWORD

W e are surrounded by and located within all sorts of networks: from our families, coworkers, and fellow believers in our local church, to TV and radio networks, computer networks, the *Internet*.

Of course, these days the noun *network* is often used as a verb: *networking*. We network with our friends and potential clients, with local politicians and professional collaborators. And many people have strong opinions about networking in this sense. Enthusiasts may subsist on the advice of their favorite networking guru, while others treat networking with suspicion, as if it somehow dilutes the gospel or leads to manipulating others. Champions and critics alike often treat networking as if it's a recent invention, like the smartphone.

Joe Castleberry, however, shows that Christ's ministry on earth and the Holy Spirit's work in growing the kingdom of God are themselves networks. After all, Jesus tells us that the kingdom of God is like a fishnet, and tells His disciples that they will become fishers of men.

The centrality of networks and networking in the Bible may seem obvious once they have been pointed out. Just try to think of Jesus's ministry or the ministries of the apostles without seeing evidence of networking. But Castleberry goes far beyond that simple observation in the following pages. He explores the full meaning and texture of networking in Scripture and in the Christian life, and gives detailed, practical advice on how to develop the biblical principles of networks in everyday life. In doing so, he invites

Christians to serve God and others by growing and developing their networks with enthusiasm for the advance of God's kingdom.

Jay W. Richards, PhD
DISTINGUISHED FELLOW,
INSTITUTE FOR FAITH, WORK & ECONOMICS
SENIOR FELLOW, DISCOVERY INSTITUTE
CO-AUTHOR OF *NEW YORK TIMES* BEST-SELLER *INDIVISIBLE*
AUTHOR, *MONEY, GREED, AND GOD*

ACKNOWLEDGMENTS

Without the Christian business community of Seattle's Eastside, I would never have written this book. I owe an enormous debt of gratitude to kingdom networkers like Jon Sharpe, Jeff Rogers, Phil Vallerand, Tim Knapp, each of the people mentioned in this book, and dozens of other friends who have shown me how it works and who understand it better than I do. They have been my instructors in Christ.

In 1 Corinthians 4:15, Paul said: "For though you might have ten thousand instructors in Christ, yet you do not have many fathers" (NKJV). I have already mentioned Jesse Owens as one of my "fathers in Christ." Here I owe special thanks to Ted Terry, my *pater libri* who works so hard to get publishers to look at my efforts. My own father, the sainted James J. Castleberry, could not have been more zealous to help me!

Thanks also to Steve Blount of Influence Resources, who was willing to take a chance on the book and to Terri Gibbs and her terrific team. My editor, Steve Halliday, deserves a medal for working with me on this project. I am also grateful to Don Detrick, Kay Owens, and Steven Gandara who read early versions of the manuscript and offered helpful advice. My gratitude also belongs to Dr. George O. Wood, who serves as the finest role model I could hope for in my profession as a minister. I also owe a debt to Northwest University for giving me the platform that allows me to make so many friends throughout the Northwest, across the country, and around the world.

My family is a constant source of joy. My wife, Kathleen, is the single greatest encouragement to my writing efforts. My daughters Jessica, Jodie, and Sophie are similar in motivating me to accomplish as much as I can.

INTRODUCTION

I often hear people make disparaging comments about networking. Sometimes, they see networking as a selfish activity—perhaps someone networks in order to create sales targets or to make friends who can help them climb a career ladder. While there is nothing inherently wrong with either ambition or profit, such critics make a good point: networking can indeed serve selfish pursuits.

On the other hand, none of us can do without networking if we want to succeed in life. Through networking, we meet new people, establish a connection with them, learn what they need and want, and figure out how to cooperate for mutual benefit. Why create products or offer services if no one wants them? And how can we know how to serve people without first learning what they need? By networking, we create ties to others who can benefit from the products and services we have to offer. Just as we can use networking for selfish gain, so can we use it to create a highway for serving others. And sometimes, friendship breaks out!

The greatest networker in history was Jesus Christ. Beginning with a team of three close friends and a dozen followers, He created an organization that today has over 2 billion members. The number of people who follow Jesus "has nearly quadrupled in the last 100 years, from about 600 million in 1910 to more than 2 billion in 2010." [1] No one has ever built a larger personal social network, and no one has ever called Jesus selfish!

Jesus networked for a single purpose: to introduce people to the kingdom of God. No product, service, or personal friendship can meet the needs of people more completely than ushering them into God's rule. Jesus used networking to deliver to humanity the highest level of service that anyone has ever offered.

Regardless of your line of work, adopting the Jesus style of networking can take your life and career to a new level. By networking His way, you can achieve greater success in your career or professional life. You can enhance your personal life through building more and better friendships. You can find more significance in your life by ratcheting up the level and breadth of service you provide to others, whether at work, play, or rest. As you do so, you will find that you draw nearer to God as well.

Many people don't purposefully engage in networking because they don't know how or where to start. Perhaps as many as half of us are introverts, who don't naturally connect with people as easily as "social butterflies" do. [2] You may feel anxious about networking, or you may have a great desire to enhance your performance as a networker. Either way, learning to network like Jesus will help you make the most of your life for God and for others. In the process, you will find that you feel more motivated than ever to become a kingdom networker. And you'll know where to start.

Think of *The Kingdom Net* as a holistic approach to networking. I want to give you a whole new way of *thinking* about networking, of *imitating* great models of networking, and of *doing* effective networking. I hope that by giving you such a full-orbed look at networking, what you learn here will stay with you a long time and will radically improve, broaden, and strengthen your whole approach to networking—for your benefit and for God's glory.

So whenever you see a chapter marked "Think," get ready to ponder deeply some crucial aspects of the kingdom that will help you lay a solid foundation for a successful life of networking. Whenever you see a chapter marked "Imitate," prepare to observe how one of God's master networkers has operated; note what that person did, and try to imitate it. And whenever you see a chapter marked "Do," that's your chance to gain some real-world tips on putting into practice strategies and tactics that will help you to become an effective networker. You'll find all three kinds of chapters interspersed throughout the book. I've done this purposefully to help you build a solid understanding and an effective practice of networking that will serve you well for a lifetime.

In addition, each chapter in the book includes exercises called "Working the Net" that are designed to help you make the most of your personal and professional networks for God's kingdom. Take time to write down answers to the questions in a private notebook or diary.

Finally, after you finish this book, you will understand the kingdom of God—and your everyday role in it—in a whole new way. You will have gained practical tools to make your life more people-centered, more interconnected, more successful, and more spiritually fruitful than ever before. May God bless you as you take up the net!

CHAPTER ONE

THE PARABLE OF THE KINGDOM NET

Matthew 13:47–50 says "The kingdom of heaven is like a net that was let down into the lake and caught all kinds of fish. When it was full, the fishermen pulled it up on the shore. Then they sat down and collected the good fish in baskets, but threw the bad away."

The kingdom of God, Jesus said, is like a net. That figurative saying has special meaning in today's world of Internet, Facebook, Twitter, Pinterest, Instagram, Classmates.com, emailing, texting, and other social networking tools. Unlike many languages, English has a specific word for net-like relational connections: the word *network*. Since networks describe metaphorical nets rather than literal ones, we could accurately understand Jesus to say, "The kingdom of God is a network." As a matter of fact, I like to call the kingdom of God the "kingdom net."

According to Jesus, the kingdom is God's net cast into the world. Notice that the net catches both good fish and bad. Sincere and insincere people, true believers and faithless fellow travelers, all find themselves caught up in it. The kingdom of God brings in a lot of people and, as we will see later, some of them become part of the network itself. In the end, God will sort out who belongs and who doesn't.

Like New Testament-era fishermen working their nets, God constantly works the kingdom net—weaving it larger, mending its torn places, catching more fish. If the people of God make up an essential part of God's kingdom, and if the kingdom is God's net, and if the net catches good and bad fish, then what are we? Are we the net or the fish?

In fact, we are both.

No analogy is perfect, and the fact that an analogy breaks down at some point doesn't rob it of all meaning. We are both net *and* fish. In another parable-like saying, Jesus once told His disciples, "Come, follow me, and I will send you out to fish for people." [3] The disciples of Jesus Christ serve as His fishers—in effect, the network He deploys to catch more people. So in this saying, we are both the caught and the catchers. As Jesus exercises His rule in us, we begin to do His works.

GREATER WORKS

As Jesus prepared to leave His disciples to return to the Father, He promised that they would do "greater works" than He had done. [4] What a dramatic thing for Jesus to say! What did He mean? He certainly didn't mean that we would do a work greater than the one He did on the cross, the greatest work ever performed. All the good works ever done by humanity combined do not equal it and cannot substitute for it. So clearly, He did not mean *that*.

It also seems very unlikely that Jesus meant we would do miracles of more impressive quality than the ones He did. He performed dramatic miracles of every kind, the greatest among them, perhaps, when He called Lazarus out of his tomb three days after his burial. While the disciples of Jesus have certainly raised more people from the dead than Jesus did during His physical life on earth, we can't say that the raising of one life is any greater than the raising of another. Neither does the healing of one sick person overshadow the healing of another.

Jesus meant that His disciples would do more miracles and evangelize more people and win more souls than He had done during His physical life on earth. And in fact, the disciples of Jesus have carried on His works for twenty full centuries since His death, and the numerical tally of their miracles and their "fishing results" vastly exceeds the total number of people Jesus touched during His life on earth. Of course, Jesus deserves all of the credit for our accomplishments since He performed them all through us. And so He will reap all the profits. After all, we are His fishing company. The big one that got away, the little ones we almost let slip through the net, the fish

> **JESUS MEANT THAT HIS DISCIPLES WOULD DO MORE MIRACLES AND EVANGELIZE MORE PEOPLE AND WIN MORE SOULS THAN HE HAD DONE DURING HIS PHYSICAL LIFE ON EARTH.**

we caught and delivered to His shore—all the "net profits" belong to Him.

If the kingdom of God is a net, then it is primarily a fishnet. The kingdom doesn't seek to take the place of earthly governments or businesses or the family or schools or labor unions or hospitals or any other institution of society. The kingdom net exists to fish. Although the kingdom embraces and holds sway over every dimension of our lives, it can never truly and fully reflect the reign of God over us without engaging us in the King's quest to seek and save the lost. The kingdom net always involves reconciling lost people to the God who loves them. Kingdom networking ultimately focuses on bringing people to Jesus.

KINGS AND KINGDOMS

So what is a kingdom? First of all, a kingdom has a social dimension. On one hand, a kingdom consists of the reign of the king. Without the ruling function, no kingdom exists; it's just a bunch of people living in the same general area. Similarly, the kingdom of God exists only where God rules. When a person has not acknowledged and submitted to the rule of God—the lordship of Jesus Christ—that person remains outside of the kingdom. God has not begun to rule in that person's life, so the kingdom has not yet come there. It is precisely our confession of Christ's lordship that brings us "into Christ." [5] Once we have entered into Christ, we become new creations, He begins to exercise His lordship, and we become part of God's kingdom . . . an important part of God's enterprise in the world.

On the other hand, a kingdom means more than the mere exercise of power. Don't forget the social component of a kingdom! If you wanted to rule as king of a territory, you might move to a vast area, perhaps, let's say, the Sahara Desert. You could start building a border fence and set apart miles and miles of desert, and you could declare yourself the king of Saharaland. It wouldn't matter how many square miles of desert your fence might contain— you might fence in a territory larger than some of the world's smallest kingdoms—but none of that would make you a true king.

You become a true king only when people recognize your rule. Ruling *land* doesn't make you a king, but rather, ruling *people*. I have a pretty strong suspicion that before you got very far in your "fencing," the real potentate of the land would come with some of his subjects and run a curved sword through your pretensions. Unless you had your own subjects who would stand with you to defend your kingship, it wouldn't last long.

So a kingdom consists of at least three things: (1) a king; (2) the rule of the king; and (3) the people who accept that rule. The kingdom of God therefore begins with the kingship of Jesus,

> **"**
> **THE KINGDOM OF GOD THEREFORE BEGINS WITH THE KINGSHIP OF JESUS, FUNCTIONS THROUGH HIS DIVINE AUTHORITY, AND TAKES PLACE IN HIS RULE OVER THE PEOPLE WHO HAVE RECOGNIZED HIS ROLE AND RULE IN THEIR LIVES.**
> **"**

functions through His divine authority, and takes place in His rule over the people who have recognized His role and rule in their lives.

The concept of the kingdom of God didn't begin in the New Testament, but rather in the Hebrew Scriptures. Even before the rise of Saul's kingdom in Israel, the people of the line of Abraham, Isaac, and Jacob understood that God should rule them, not a merely human king. While that's an elegant vision, it proved unworkable in practice. Sinful human beings couldn't, in their own power, live out that blessed ideal.

With the coming of King David and the prophetic revelation that followed, the concept of God's kingdom took on a messianic shape. In God's plan, an Anointed One (the translation of the Hebraic word *messiah*, as well as the Grecian word *Christ*), full of God's Spirit, would appear among men and women and establish the kingdom of God among us. As John the Baptist came declaring the imminent coming of the kingdom, the Spirit would anoint the promised Messiah, thus fulfilling the Old Testament promises about the outpouring of God's Spirit on all flesh.

And so, with the appearance of Jesus, God declared the kingdom of God had come to humanity. Before the coming of the King, the kingdom remained incomplete. The incarnation—the birth of God as a human being—had central importance for the coming of God's kingdom. I confess I never fully understood that idea until I met a real-life king.

MEETING A KING

I have met senators and congressmen and governors and national presidents several times in my life, but I had never met a king until

I visited the tiny country of Lesotho in southern Africa. As part of my visit to an impressive rural development project operated by World Vision, I met Letsie III, King of the Basotho people.

King Letsie lives in a large palace that sits on a hill, surrounded by a rock wall and a human security force. The palace doesn't insult the Basotho people by seeming too ostentatious; rather, it honors their king with unmistakable dignity. As I prepared to meet the king, I thought hard about how to honor him without appearing ostentatious myself.

Visitors meeting dignitaries should always bring a gift. I had brought along several Northwest University coffee mugs and also a branded T-shirt. I had also learned to say a few sentences in Sesotho, the national language of King Letsie's people. (That's right. The Basotho people in Lesotho speak Sesotho.) I practiced my new language skills in my head and also thought hard about what I would say to him in English.

When attendants ushered us into the king's reception hall, our group of about a dozen people sat in chairs along the wall in a horseshoe shape. Each of us in turn had a chance to greet the king and tell him our story. When my turn came, I greeted him in Sesotho and said a couple of sentences about how honored I felt to meet him and to visit his beautiful country. He seemed pleasantly surprised that I had learned some of his native language. Switching to English, I told him who I was and why I had come to his country. I briefly described Northwest University and presented him with six coffee mugs. I hoped that he would occasionally see the mugs and think of our school. I also offered a 100 percent tuition scholarship to one young person from Lesotho whom he would choose to attend our school. Then I presented him with the T-shirt I had brought.

The shirt featured a graphic of a set of barbells and said "Northwest University Wrestling Team—Undefeated Since 1934."

After a few impressed reactions from the king and his staff, I explained our little joke; in fact, the university doesn't have a wrestling team. It has never suffered a defeat since it has never competed (which means it has never won a victory, either). I recognized that the problems of Lesotho, with an HIV-positive rate of 30 percent, were indeed a heavy weight. We knew we couldn't lift that burden alone but had come to join our efforts with World Vision and the Basotho people to win as many small victories as possible. Over time, I said, we would win the big victory together.

> **THE INCARNATION OF GOD IN THE PERSON OF JESUS CHRIST MADE IT POSSIBLE FOR GOD TO RULE HUMANITY AS ONE OF OUR OWN PEOPLE.**

I said that we would remain a joke only if we never tried. Trying and failing doesn't make one into a joke, but never wrestling with problems means never winning—and we would rather risk defeat than become a joke. The king felt moved by the gifts and accepted them with a regal display of both amusement and respect.

The dignified way in which King Letsie represented his people deeply impressed me, and I began to understand one of the basic aspects of kingship. Kings differ from presidents in a fundamental way. While all heads of state represent the people of their nations, presidents and prime ministers serve for a limited time. Kings and queens represent the whole history of their people for their whole lifetime. For thousands of years, people have customarily spoken of the coronation of a king or queen as his or her birthday. From the day of their "birth" as kings and queens, they represent the people of their nation for life. In essence, the Queen of England *is* England. The King of Norway *is* Norway. In ancient times, kings and queens called each other by the names of their countries rather than by their personal names. Kings and queens not only represent their people during the course of their lifetimes, but they represent the kings and queens who have gone before them—the embodiment of the whole history of their people. Reigning as a king or queen is a really big deal!

THE DEEP MAGIC OF KINGSHIP

Human beings have always understood what a shameful thing it is for a foreigner to rule a people. No nation on earth will tolerate it gladly. As C. S. Lewis might have said (in language from *The Lion, the Witch, and the Wardrobe*), part of the "Deep Magic" God has written into the human consciousness requires that someone from among our own people rule us. [6] This helps explain the inherently anti-Christ nature of empires. Human rulers who desire to reign over a people group not their own usurp the unique authority of Jesus Christ as the only King of kings and Lord of lords.

In short, to establish a fully legitimate kingdom, God had to take human form. The incarnation of God in the person of Jesus Christ made it possible for God to rule humanity as one of our own people. The kingdom of God could not arrive until Jesus appeared on the scene. But once Jesus had come, the first element of a kingdom fell into place. At long last, we had a universal human king, the Son of God born as the Son of Man. Because Jesus rules as the King of every nation, He is the King of kings.

In its essence, the kingdom is the rule of God, God's power in action—the second element of a kingdom. When John the Baptist landed in prison, he began to doubt whether Jesus really was the King who would restore Israel and bring about the final judgment of evil. When John sent his disciples to ask Jesus "Are you the one who is to come?" Jesus replied, "Go back and report to John what you have seen and heard: The blind receive sight, the lame walk, those who have leprosy are cleansed, the deaf hear, the dead are raised, and the good news is proclaimed to the poor." [7] In the same way, when we see Jesus healing the sick among us now, when He sets the oppressed free, when spiritually dead people kneel to the Lordship of Christ and rise up in new life, we are watching the rule of God. We are seeing God's kingdom in action.

> **NETWORKING IS PART OF THE VERY NATURE OF THE KINGDOM OF GOD.**

But the kingdom also means that people submit to the Lordship of Christ, the third element of a kingdom. When we see the people of God brought together and we sense our connection to them through the Holy Spirit who makes King Jesus present in us all, we see the kingdom. So the kingdom of God is both visible and invisible. The presence of Jesus, at work through His people, makes it visible. The parable of the net(work) portrays the kingdom not as a territory, but as a network of people.

WHY FISHERMEN?

Have you ever wondered why Jesus called so many fishermen to become His disciples? It's because they were "net-workers."

No, I'm not attempting some lame humor here. I'm serious. Fishermen were *exactly* the kind of people Jesus needed. Certainly, Jesus' disciples didn't understand many things when He chose them. None of them were great theologians, skilled writers, trained public speakers, or psychological counselors. They had received no training in any of the subjects so popular in today's seminaries. But they all had one indisputable qualification: They were networkers.

Networking is part of the very nature of the kingdom of God. At the most literal level, Peter and his friends knew how fishing nets worked. They knew how to make nets, how to cast them over the side of the boat, how to work them in the water, how to draw them back into the boat, and how to mend them and maintain them after the day's work. But they also knew something even more vital.

Running a successful fishing business in first-century Israel required more than just working nets. It also required networking. Fishermen knew not only how to work nets, but also how to work as a team. They knew how to take the fish to market and how to sell them. They knew how to find people who would transport the fish into the interior of the countryside and market them in the surrounding communities. They understood distribution, marketing, sales, profit margins, and other business aspects of their work. We would recognize them today as expert networkers.

KINGDOM NETWORKING

If you intend to fish for people, then you have to know how to operate people "nets." To operate successfully in God's kingdom, you must have good networking skills. Networking is *the* essential kingdom task; but despite this fact, seminaries don't commonly teach courses in networking. (I don't think the word ever came up during my own ten years of academic training for Christian ministry.) To be fair, the word *network* hadn't entered the vernacular by the early 1980s, except in broadcasting. But even so, how could we have overlooked such an incredibly important skill?

> **"**
> **TO OPERATE SUCCESSFULLY IN GOD'S KINGDOM, YOU MUST HAVE GOOD NETWORKING SKILLS.**
> **"**

As a college president, I serve as Networker-in-Chief for my school. I love it, since as a people-person, I delight in maintaining friendships, meeting new people, and weaving all those relationships into a broader, stronger network that we can deploy to accomplish our mission as a university. As I write, I know I also have some mending jobs to work on. Even if I didn't create the tears (you pick the pronunciation you prefer), I have a responsibility to make sure they get mended. I love my job, and I love the people-tasks it entails. I especially love the fact that the fruit of our work relates so directly to the mission of God's kingdom.

But my job holds no patent on networking. Any follower of Jesus, regardless of his or her work, can express the kingdom of God through networking.

WORKING THE NET

1. All kingdom networking begins with prayer. Think of the Lord's Prayer as a great network tool, a cry for God's kingdom to come— that is, for God's will to be done in our lives. If you don't recite the Lord's Prayer every day, you may want to consider doing so in a thoughtful and reflective way. Kingdom networkers should reflect every day on God's kingly rule. Take time to thoughtfully say the Lord's Prayer now, thinking about each of the petitions as it relates to your life today:

> Our Father in heaven,
> hallowed be your name,
> your kingdom come,
> your will be done, on earth as it is in heaven.
> Give us today our daily bread.
> And forgive us our debts, as we also have forgiven
> our debtors.
> And lead us not into temptation,
> but deliver us from the evil one. [8]

2. In your personal life outside of your job, who are the closest people in your network? Pray that God will reign in their lives and will meet their needs. If you need to forgive one of these individuals, submit the offense to God and begin to forgive. Pray that he or she may overcome temptation and sin.

3. Who are the individuals closest to you in your work with whom you network? Pray for them as you have prayed for those in your

personal life. Pray that they will submit to and reap the benefits of God's kingly rule.

4. Write down the names of three people you need to meet in order to achieve some good result. Pray that God will help you to connect with them and that you may be able to serve them through your networking.

5. If you don't have a regular prayer list, consider downloading a smart-phone app such as "My Prayer Lists" or "7:14 Prayer" or another one that fits your needs. If you don't have a smart phone, just keep a list on the notepad feature of your cell phone. Keeping your prayer list in your phone guarantees that you won't lose it and also keeps it private.

CHAPTER TWO

IMITATE

JESUS AND THE KINGDOM NET

G od has determined that the kingdom should flourish through the efforts of Jesus' followers working the kingdom net. In this chapter, we will look at how Jesus began to weave and work the net that quickly covered the earth. In particular, we will investigate the Jesus way of networking as described in the gospel of Luke. [9]

NETWORKING AND THE EARLY LIFE OF JESUS

While the Gospels make it clear that Jesus didn't begin to declare the coming of the kingdom until He reached the age of thirty, the events described in Luke's gospel give us a unique opportunity to look into the networking related to the birth of Jesus and His childhood. Even before Jesus' birth, the network of people who would become devoted to Christ began to form when Zechariah, a temple priest, and Elizabeth, Mary's cousin, welcomed a son after many years of childless marriage.

The angel Gabriel appeared to Zechariah and revealed that his miracle son would become a great prophet—thread one. Six months later, Gabriel also appeared to Mary to announce that she would become pregnant and bear a Son, the promised Messiah—thread two. When the two women met to compare notes shortly after Mary's experience, the Holy Spirit came upon Elizabeth also, filling her and the child within her. Mary stayed with Elizabeth for three months until the birth of John the Baptist. And so the first two threads came together and formed the first knot in the kingdom net.

NETWORKING TIP

There is no networking like the kind the
Holy Spirit weaves among believers.

The kingdom cannot exist in a person until the Holy Spirit comes upon him or her. [10] Not even the shared visits by Gabriel linked Mary and Elizabeth as powerfully as did the visitation of the Holy Spirit on both of them when they met. God thought it essential that these two women come together to share their divine experiences. Both had experienced an angelic visit from Gabriel; both had become miraculously pregnant; both had known the powerful filling of the Holy Spirit. Together they had become the first hearers of the good news of Christ.

Note here the crucial fact that God's kingdom net began with a family relationship. God chose to use close cousins, Elizabeth and Mary, to create the first kingdom cell group. They simply couldn't bear alone the magnitude of the news they had received. They needed family around to help them.

You can certainly work the kingdom net even if you're the only believer in your family, but what a priceless blessing you have when family members share and understand the call God has placed on you! Just ask George W. Bush or Anne Graham Lotz—prominent leaders today whose family connections gave their talent and calling a running start.

NETWORKING TIP

A godly family heritage can serve as a powerful foundation for your vocational network.

With the birth of Jesus, the kingdom net immediately began to acquire new threads. The angelic band wove shepherds from the fields around Bethlehem into the net, calling them to attend the manger scene and support the holy family with joy and wonder. The Bible never tells us anything more about the shepherds, and in worldly terms, they had little importance, since only children, hirelings, or slaves worked as shepherds. [11] They certainly lacked the impressive stature of the Magi, whom Matthew reported as early visitors to the holy family. Nevertheless, they received the word of the Messiah's birth with joy, and it seems highly probable that some of them became followers of Jesus' ministry when both He and they grew older.

As the eminent New Testament scholar James Charlesworth once pointed out to me, one can hardly read the teachings of Jesus without concluding that He spent some time with shepherds (or even worked as a shepherd) over the course of His life. [12] Could Jesus' network have started on the day shepherds came to worship Him? Could some of those shepherds have kept track of Him and even had a part in teaching Him much of what He knew about flocks and their care?

NETWORKING TIP

Never underestimate the importance of "unimportant" people in the kingdom net.

The humblest person you meet can become extremely important to your future success. During the time I lived overseas, I knew an important leader whom I once irritated by referring to his wife as his *señora*. I thought it sounded respectful and elegant, a correct assumption in my culture. But it wounded his ego, since *señora* not only means "Mrs." but also implies authority, meaning "lady" in the sense of "lords and ladies." He immediately corrected me: "She's not my *señora*, she's my *esposa* (wife)." While I considered him a good man in many ways, he was a terrible sexist: no woman would lord it over him! While no one ever called him a humble man, he did owe his soul to a humble man. In fact, his gardener, a poor and uneducated man, led him to faith in Christ by his humble example and irreproachable life. An "unimportant person" turned out to be the most important person this man ever met.

Perhaps I should suggest here that you avoid getting too gender-focused in your networking. The most effective networking includes both men and women. The cultivation of relationships exclusively within your gender has many serious weaknesses. It creates huge holes in your personal network and may result in unjust treatment of others—shutting out either men or women from the benefits you can offer them, while also depriving you of what they can offer you. Jesus carefully cultivated healthy relationships with women, and both they and He benefitted.

Of course, people stumble over more than gender prejudice. Many look down on older people, poor people, people of other races, and people whose usefulness or value they question. Many individuals consider children unimportant. But knowing and serving the children of other people—whether they seem "important" or otherwise—can result in the gain of powerful influence. While serving the children of powerful people can seem "useful," take care that you have the right motivation. Children and teenagers can detect a phony by pure instinct; and in any case, you do not want to "use" people's children to get their attention. Serve people, especially children, because they need you, not to gain benefit for yourself.

The kingdom net also reserves an important place for older people. Jesus' circumcision at the temple in Jerusalem brought Simeon and Anna into the web of support that Jesus' parents needed. These two superannuated prophets had both received word of the coming of the Messiah in their lifetimes, and the Holy Spirit moved both of them to go to the temple to speak God's word of confirmation to Mary and Joseph.

The experience, wisdom, enhanced spiritual depth, and ongoing relational connections of older believers can make them important nodes in the kingdom net. Anna and Simeon provided an important affirmation of the reality of Mary's mission of bearing and raising the Messiah.

Mary's connection with Anna and Simeon may have lasted only a few moments, but the memory of it lasted forever. We can never measure the value of a missional relationship in terms of money, duration, or the number of other relationships it weaves into our lives. We must never reduce kingdom networking to a utilitarian enterprise. In other words, kingdom networking doesn't depend on any linear or rational evaluation of usefulness. People have value in their own right, and the effect of divine appointments doesn't always follow a linear progression or look mutually obvious to the people involved. At times, a chance encounter with someone can change your life (or theirs) in an eternal way, even if you never see them again or learn about the impact you had on them. Whether you bless them or they bless you, friendly fellowship among human beings is delightful and pleases God.

Our encounters with people become part of our memory network, even if we never see the individuals again. I once met President Jimmy Carter at Princeton University, and I doubt whether I will ever meet him again. But networking doesn't have to create long-term, close relationships to have long-term value. My meeting with the president became a story that I share when I meet others who have also met Jimmy Carter, and our shared experience often gets us off to a great conversation that has the potential to build over time into beneficial cooperation.

The stories of Jesus' childhood in Luke and Matthew (the other Gospels contain none) tell us little about His personal networking style, but Luke does tell us about Jesus' first attempt at networking. When He was twelve years old, His family left the small town of Nazareth and attended the Passover Feast in Jerusalem, something they apparently did every year. [13] After the festivities, Jesus' parents, confused about His whereabouts, left for home without Him.

As anyone who has seen the movie *Home Alone* can tell you, a boy left alone can demonstrate a great deal of ingenuity. [14] Jesus was no exception, except for His totally exceptional nature. Momentarily free from parental oversight, He went to work on building His network. For three days, He spent time with the Jerusalem rabbis, listening to them and asking (and answering!) precocious questions. As the Bible says, "Everyone who heard him was amazed at his understanding and his answers." [15] We can assume that Jesus' interaction with the Jerusalem rabbis didn't end after His return to daily life in Nazareth, since, as He told His parents, He had to take care of His Father's business. (The Greek New Testament literally says, "It is necessary for me to be in the things of my Father.")

*It's never too early to begin establishing a relationship with
authorities and experts in the field of your calling.*

I have a pastor friend who excels as an effective networker. His
brilliant teenage son wants to become a scholar and theologian, so
his father has begun to introduce him to world-famous people in
the field of religion, apologetics, theology, ethics, and ministry. By
the age of sixteen, this young man had already met more prominent
religious authorities than I had in the first forty years of my life.
Even if he doesn't establish long-term relationships with those
leaders, he is gaining confidence and poise and now understands
that he belongs in the room with anyone. Jesus must have felt the
same way after successfully dialoguing and networking with the
Jerusalem rabbis, the most highly regarded authorities on Judaism
in the world.

LAUNCHING OUT

As Jesus reached the age of thirty, He was ready in every way to
launch His ministry as a rabbi. At His baptism by the hand of John
the Baptist, the voice of the Father declared Jesus to be the Son
of God, and the Holy Spirit drove Him into the wilderness to be
tempted by the Devil. After defeating temptation in the desert, Jesus
returned to society and began to preach in the local synagogues,
"being glorified by all." [16] But not for long; trouble began when He
showed up in the synagogue in Nazareth, His hometown, to read

the Scriptures. Things got a bit dicey when He announced that His presence fulfilled the "year of the Lord's favor," the messianic age itself. [17] The people of the city rose up to kill Him, accusing Him of blasphemy. So we can assume the event didn't go down as a great networking success.

What went wrong? Everyone in Nazareth knew Jesus as a brilliant interpreter of the Scriptures. Word of His consultation with the rabbis in Jerusalem no doubt spread widely (word travels fast in such places!). While the people of Nazareth allowed Him to read and interpret the Scriptures, they wanted Him to do a few miracles at home, as He had done in nearby Capernaum. [18] They refused, however, to accept him as the Messiah. Jesus then stated a general principle that applies widely to kingdom networkers: "No prophet is accepted in his hometown." [19]

NETWORKING TIP

Like Jesus, many highly effective networkers will have to leave their hometowns to achieve great results in the kingdom net.

While family relationships can provide powerful help in networking, they can also stunt the growth of budding leaders. Roles established among school friends can limit the development of leaders, so leaving town after high school—whether for college or work or foreign missions or other service—can break young leaders out of the habitual patterns that cause them to underestimate their leadership capabilities. They may not have earned the label "Most Likely to Succeed" in school, but the calling of God doesn't depend on such juvenile things. Sometimes you have to leave home to begin building the network that will lead to future effectiveness in living out your call to ministry, business, professional life, or marriage.

Leaving town for a few years doesn't mean you can never go back. Often, you can go away for a few years, build some links to the outside world, and then return home. The network built in the wide world then becomes a source of new ideas, help for projects, counsel during difficult situations, and an outlet for temporary escape. Few businesses can survive on a purely local level; the same holds true for churches. Professional practice also requires links to a broader world. Successful political careers usually involve a careful weaving of networks—locally and in the county seat, in the state capital or other major cities, and in the national capital. Whether you plan to live a strictly local life or a highly mobile and cosmopolitan one, you must network outside your home territory if you want to become all that you can be for God's kingdom.

BUILDING A NETWORK OF DISCIPLES

As Jesus moved from building His personal network to building His "organization," He recognized the necessity of attracting talented candidates for the future leadership of His enterprise. He needed people who could serve His mission not only for the short term but for the long haul. His own public career wouldn't last long, just three years, before He would finish His saving work on the cross and ascend to the Father to rule forever as King. The people who would choose to walk with Him as disciples would become the networkers who would spread the experience of His lordship by working the kingdom net.

The people He chose back then illustrate valuable concepts for contemporary kingdom networkers. Simon, a bold and manly person, had both physical strength and a taste for action. The gospel of Mark (according to tradition, based on Peter's remembrance of Jesus) repeatedly uses the word *euthus* ("straight away," "immediately"). Simon saw Jesus as a man of action like him, but also as a man unlike him, both holy and perfect. So he chose to give up everything to follow Jesus and become more like Him. While Simon lacked a formal education, [20] Jesus saw him as one who could become a fearless, resolute leader. And so Jesus gave him a nickname that would stick in both Greek and Aramaic: *Petros* (Greek) and *Cephas* (Aramaic). Both names mean "Rocky." While Peter's relationship with Jesus grew rocky in the wrong way at times, Jesus knew that Peter would grow to become firm and unmovable, and so declared that He would build His church upon such people. In its early unfolding, the kingdom would need just such individuals as Peter at strategic moments.

NETWORKING TIP

People of action are necessary to accomplish any good work.

Simon Peter's brother, Andrew, had a different kind of personality. Like Peter, he, too, worked as a fisherman, a strong and manly person. His name even means "manly." [21] But Andrew apparently had a more religious bent than Peter. The gospel of John reveals that Andrew had followed John the Baptist before he became a disciple of Jesus. [22] He and John the son of Zebedee were the first two people to follow Jesus. His actions in the New Testament reveal him as an ideal "first follower." In a terrific video about how movements get started, Derek Sivers points out that the "first follower" turns a person out of sync with the crowd into a leader. [23] And as John Maxwell has said, if you think you are leading, but have no one following, you are only taking a walk! [24]

NETWORKING TIP

The first followers or "early joiners" are crucial in drawing people to the leader of a new movement.

Andrew took up his role immediately, going to his brother Simon Peter to encourage him to follow Jesus. Later in Jesus' ministry, Andrew introduced the Lord to a boy who offered to share his lunch of "five barley loaves and two fish," an event that facilitated the miracle of the feeding of the 5,000. [25] His networking on another occasion communicated to Jesus the desire of several God-fearing Greeks (or Grecian Jews) to meet Him during their time of worship in Jerusalem. [26] While Simon Peter was a man of action, Jesus saw Andrew as a natural people-person who would become an effective weaver of the kingdom net.

Jesus called James and John the "Sons of Thunder," and on one occasion He had to rebuke them for urging Him to let them call down fire from heaven to consume a Samaritan village. [27] These fishermen lacked both refinement and education, but they had plenty of ambition. They asked Jesus to make them His top lieutenants in the kingdom and even sent their mother (perhaps Jesus' aunt) to ask Him the same question. [28] Fiery of nature and loud of presence, ambitious for authority but apparently undisciplined, they needed significant spiritual shaping. But it takes far less effort to calm down a fiery, ambitious person than it does to fire up a lazy one!

Jesus saw potential in James and John, and they didn't disappoint Him. James became one of the first martyrs, boldly preaching the gospel and making noise in Jerusalem about the kingdom. [29]

These two brothers, like Peter and Andrew, had contrasting personalities. John seems to have been the more spiritual of the two. He went on to become "the disciple Jesus loved," lived into deep old age, and wrote the gospel and epistles of John and the book of Revelation. [30] He displayed a deep love for people, and his message to the churches of Asia Minor consistently called them to love one another. [31] Jesus chose well in including John in His network.

Matthew (also called Levi) worked as a tax collector at the time Jesus called him. The fact that Jesus chose him demonstrates an impressive ability to see beyond a person's immediate circumstances. As a tax collector, Matthew demonstrated no shame, collaborating openly with the Roman Empire to oppress the Jewish people. The Jewish population put tax collectors and prostitutes on the same moral plain, since both prostituted themselves to the Romans, selling their dignity for money. Still, Jesus saw past Matthew's degrading profession and perceived what he could become in another, more appropriate imperial role—a networker in the kingdom of God. Jesus had come to seek and save the lost, and He rescued Matthew from his service of evil, putting his skills to far better use. [32]

The same abilities that made it possible for Matthew to collect taxes and keep records became extremely valuable in the kingdom of God. The early church father Papias recorded that Matthew went on to "compile the sayings of Jesus in Hebrew," a compilation preserved in the gospel of Matthew. [33] Luke 5:29 records some of Matthew's networking for the kingdom, telling of the great feast he held at his house in Jesus' honor. Like the other tax collector, Zacchaeus (described in Luke 10), Matthew used his large home and the wealth he had accumulated in wrongdoing to honor Jesus and introduce Him to his friends. While Jesus had no home of His own, He recognized the value of people with open homes.

NETWORKING TIP

People with money who willingly open their homes can wield considerable influence in any kind of networking.

We know less about Philip than we do about many of the other disciples, but he seems to have had a strong acquaintance with the Scriptures. [34] That would set him apart from the fishermen. On two occasions, he brought others to Jesus to introduce them to Him. Nothing can substitute for having knowledgeable people around, and if they can also network effectively, they can exercise significant influence through both their expertise and their sociability.

NETWORKING TIP

Any leader would do well to cultivate studious people who also know how to network.

Nathanael seems to have been a careful person who initially doubted Philip's declaration of Jesus as the Messiah. But Jesus, upon meeting Nathanael, immediately recognized him as a person of noble character and greeted him as a true Israelite, "in whom there is no deceit." [35] While Nathanael was a thinker, he was no skeptic. As a strong believer in God, he wanted to know the truth. Jesus proved Himself to Nathanael, saying that He had seen him "under the fig tree." [36] We can only guess why this revelation impressed Nathanael so much, and apparently it surprised even Jesus to see how easily he became convinced. Nathanael immediately recognized Jesus with the words, "Rabbi, you are the Son of God; you are the king of Israel!" [37] While some thinking people can become paralyzed through their analysis, unable to adopt a new idea and move into action, Nathanael leapt in with both feet.

Careful thinkers who can avoid the trap of analysis paralysis can become powerful players in any network.

While Nathanael avoided becoming a skeptic, it appears that Thomas had turned into one by the time of Jesus' death. We know little about Thomas beyond the fact that he was a twin. Both his Aramaic name *Thomas* and his Greek name *Didymus* mean "twin." Tradition identifies his given name as Judas. [38] John 11:14–16 suggests that he may have had a gloomy nature. When Jesus announced that Lazarus had died and that he would go to him, Thomas replied, "Let us also go, that we may die with him." The text doesn't make it clear whether he means, "let's go die with Jesus" or "let's go die like Lazarus did." Perhaps he understood Jesus' words, "Lazarus has died, . . . but let us go to him," to mean what David had said of his deceased child: "now that he is dead . . . I will go to him, but he will not return to me." [39] In either case, Thomas didn't speak the most faith-filled, hopeful words.

We all know Thomas' main claim to fame: his declaration that he wouldn't believe in Jesus' resurrection until he could put his finger in Jesus' wounds. As it turned out, he needed only to see Jesus in His post-resurrection glory to cry out in faith, "My Lord and my God." [40] He appears to have had a pessimistic and skeptical nature, but we should remember him by more than the term "doubting Thomas." He became a bold believer and went on to found the church in South India, becoming one of the most effective evangelists among the twelve.

Hard-to-convince people can become the greatest promoters of a cause after they have made their commitment.

We shouldn't forget Judas Iscariot, also one of the Twelve. Jesus discerned Judas' heart from the beginning and knew Judas would betray Him. Such a person, it turned out, had a necessary part to play in the bitter road Jesus had to walk at the end of His ministry. While you should never choose to include an evil, deceitful, traitorous person in your network of close associates, you should always remember Judas.

NETWORKING TIP

You probably have a person in your network who would betray you for the right price.

Since people don't always lay their cards on the table, you can never really tell who may sell you out. At the same time, you can't afford to become a suspicious, paranoid person. I tend to stretch out my hand of fellowship to as many people as may want to grasp it, and run the risk that some people may betray me. Some have. But the pain of betrayal is part of the cost of doing business, especially kingdom business. We might as well accept it and develop a tough hide to protect a soft heart.

We know only a little about the other men whom Jesus numbered among the Twelve. One of them, Simon the Canaanite, also carried the name "Zealot"—and if he was indeed a Zealot with a capital Z, he would have participated in a violent political revolutionary movement, perhaps representing a person capable of what we might call terrorism today. In our own day, a number of former terrorists have turned to follow Jesus and now have a passion for Christ equal to that which drove them in their prior lives. Jesus made room in His closest circle for people of fiery passion who could have their zeal harnessed for a movement—in this case, for God's kingdom.

NETWORKING TIP

Having a few passionate people in your network has great value.

Make sure you don't miss one of the really interesting things about the whole group, namely, its web of family connections. Peter and Andrew were brothers, as were James and John. Salome, the mother of James and John, apparently was the sister of Mary, the mother of Jesus, which would make the Sons of Thunder the first cousins of Jesus. Levi (Matthew), the son of Alphaeus, may have been the brother of James, the son of Alphaeus. Philip and Nathanael are mentioned together, which may indicate either a family relationship or close friendship. [41]

Jesus unquestionably used family ties to fulfill the prophecy that through Abraham all the families of the earth would be blessed. [42]

*Family connections are a natural beginning
in any kind of networking.*

INSTITUTIONS AND THE KINGDOM NET

After people in Jesus' hometown tried to kill Him for His sermon in their synagogue, you might think He would avoid synagogues or religious people. But in fact, He went down to Capernaum and visited another synagogue where He taught for a few weeks. You might say, "Well, they were a nicer group of people," but apparently they were not:

> In the synagogue there was a man possessed by a demon, an impure spirit. He cried out at the top of his voice, "Go away! What do you want with us, Jesus of Nazareth? Have you come to destroy us? I know who you are—the Holy One of God!" "Be quiet!" Jesus said sternly. "Come out of him!" Then the demon threw the man down before them all and came out without injuring him. [43]

It would seem that some unseemly folks hang out at church!

It has become popular in recent years to speak ill of religion in general, especially of that awful bugbear, "organized religion." Unquestionably, some people in our churches have "a religious spirit." Such people love to use religious observance and status within organizations to establish their power over others and make them feel inferior. They hang out in religious organizations like bats in a cave, and we should avoid them whenever possible. But no one should write off organized religion just because some religious freaks feel attracted to it. Should someone called to serve in politics write off politics because of hypocritical and dirty politicians? Should someone else write off a calling as a teacher because a few pedophiles lurk in schools? In our world, we have sick doctors, lying lawyers, abusive fathers, and church people with a religious spirit. Corruption in human institutions, however, doesn't mean that we should write off politics, schools, hospitals, the court system, the family, or churches. Every human institution suffers from corruption, because every human institution has humans in it. Although I'd love to think churches are the exception, they're not.

NETWORKING TIP

Institutions are necessary for human life to flourish.

Jesus had too much wisdom to write off synagogues simply because they harbored a few demon-possessed people. Churches play a crucial part in the kingdom net, as do other forms of organized religion. Christian universities, such as Northwest University, and Christian publishers, such as NavPress and Influence Resources, connect the kingdom through ideas. Christian compassion agencies, such as World Vision or Mercy Ships, and foreign missions boards weave the church together across national borders. Campus Ministries, such as InterVarsity or Chi Alpha or

CRU (formerly known as Campus Crusade for Christ), connect emerging leaders to Christ and to each other. Prison ministries, such as Prison Fellowship, turn bondage into an opportunity for kingdom bonding. Other such agencies of "organized religion" can play a powerful role in weaving the kingdom net.

People who oppose "organized religion" essentially say, "I'm committed to being spiritual on a personal level, but I don't believe in being committed to and cooperating with other people in a spiritual way." That attitude may work for mystics who practice postmodernist spiritualities, but it simply doesn't work for God's kingdom net. As I once said spontaneously while preaching in a chapel service for employees of World Vision, "the kingdom of God is a team sport."

NETWORKING TIP

The kingdom of God is a team sport.

The Lord's Prayer neatly illustrates the community nature of the kingdom. After saying, "your kingdom come, your will be done," the prayer adds, "give *us* today our daily bread. And forgive *us our* debts . . . , and lead *us* not into temptation, but deliver *us* from the evil one." [44] If we want to pray as Jesus taught us to pray, then we need to pray together with others. Whether we pray in the physical presence of other Christians or pray alone in solidarity with them, the Lord's Prayer sees community as an essential element of the kingdom net.

As Jesus cast out the demon that afflicted the man in the Capernaum synagogue, the center of community life for the town leaders, word traveled fast about His authority, drawing attention to His cause. Apparently, Peter heard about Jesus at that time. Jesus continued doing miracles, including the healing of Peter's mother-in-law, and as He cast out demons, many of them came out crying, "You are the Son of God." Jesus kept preaching, meeting more and more people—and meeting their needs. He ranged out of Galilee down into Judea and back again. Public success is a powerful motor for building a personal network.

NETWORKING TIP

The more influence your talents create, the more people will be attracted to you and the more people will want to introduce you to their friends.

IT TAKES ALL KINDS

As God cast the kingdom net into the world at the birth of Jesus, waves began to spread out. Beginning with the family of Jesus, the influence of the kingdom started with a very small circle. The waves grew larger and larger until they crossed the seas and covered the planet. Today, billions know the name of Jesus. The names of His earliest disciples grace churches, universities, hospitals, charities, and enterprises of every kind. Even a coffee shop in my city bears the name of St. James. As Jesus called the first disciples to weave and wield His network into theirs, He chose an amazingly strong and effective team.

Each one of the disciples brought specific strengths to the nascent network. Their personalities, relationship, talents, energy, drive, and faith guaranteed the spread of the kingdom to much of Europe, Asia, and Africa—all in the course of a single lifespan. In valuing their diversity of potentials, Jesus made clear that every kind of person and every type of skill adds value and utility to the kingdom net.

As you weave into the kingdom net around you, be sure not to limit yourself to associating only with people like yourself. To accomplish your calling, you will need the support of friends with lots of different talents and traits. And just as importantly, they will need you.

WORKING THE NET

1. Jesus included a diversity of personality types and social statuses among the disciples who made up the core of His network. These kinds of people can add strength or value to your network. Go through each of the categories below and consider who in your network of friends and friendly acquaintances would fit in each category.

Personality/Social Type	People in Your Network Who Fit
Relatives	_____
Eminences in Your Field	_____
People of Action	_____
Early Joiners	_____
Loud and Fiery	_____
People Lovers	_____
Wealthy	_____
Economically Challenged	_____
Studious	_____
Careful Thinker	_____

2. If your circle lacks any of these types of people, who could you get to know who exemplifies those personality and social types? Make a list of ten people with whom you would like to connect. Later, we will refer back to that list.

3. Make a call-list of the twelve people you know well who seem most important to your professional success. Give them a brief phone

call over the next week to say thank-you for the role they play in your work. Ask them if you can do anything to serve them.

4. Of all the networking tips in this chapter, pick the three concepts that resonated most deeply with you (or startled, or convicted you). For each of the three concepts, write out a sentence describing a concrete step you can take to put that tip to work in your life. Then do it!

CHAPTER THREE

DO

MEETING PEOPLE

he key to effective fishing is to know where the fish are.
People are everywhere, so you always want to have your
net gear with you.

Every area of professional practice, as well as everyday life, has
its own ways of getting people together, so we can't cover them all.
But we can consider some essential types of places where anyone
can meet new people who may become valuable additions to
their network. More importantly, the new connections can prove
extremely valuable for the work of God's kingdom.

The Holy Spirit plays a crucial role in working the kingdom
net. Anyone can engage in networking, and some people have more
skill in meeting people than others; but the kingdom networker
has a special advantage. God knows who we should meet and who
should get involved in our lives and work. God knows who we
can connect with others for their mutual benefit. When Christians
"accidentally" meet someone who "just so happens" to fill a great

need in their lives or in the work they seek to bless, we often call it a "divine appointment." When we walk in the Spirit, God often shows us the people we need to connect with. As you go out to network for the kingdom, never forget the One who directs the whole thing. Pray that the Holy Spirit will help you connect to the right people in doing God's will. And then go out and experience the amazing kingdom net.

WHERE TO NETWORK

Place number one for meeting people: a local church. I believe every Christian needs to become a faithful and committed member of a congregation, which includes working hard in the church's ministry and making friends with everyone possible at that church. Even people who have no commitment to Christ recognize churches as incredibly good places to meet people. Men and women used to go to church whether they had sincere faith or not, just to take advantage of the social opportunities and entertainment that churches provide. They are still wise to do so, though it seems that fewer and fewer unbelievers take advantage of what churches can offer.

> **" I BELIEVE EVERY CHRISTIAN NEEDS TO BECOME A FAITHFUL AND COMMITTED MEMBER OF A CONGREGATION. "**

From time to time, plan to visit the churches your friends attend. Having friends in other churches does good things for both congregations and pastors. When I was a child, my parents liked to support the revival meetings of other churches by attending a few weekday services at those churches. Not many churches have special revival meetings these days, but all churches have special events. If you attend a church that doesn't have special services during Holy Week or on Christmas Day or Christmas Eve, go visit other churches that do, and meet their members.

Service clubs and organizations like the Rotary Club, Kiwanis International, Civitan International, Jaycees, and the Lions Clubs International provide another incredible venue for building your network. Rotary Club, the granddaddy of them all, does wonderful work while providing awesome opportunities for leaders, both young and old, to connect with each other. Almost all towns have one or more of these clubs. Ask around and figure out which one offers you the best opportunity to engage in serving others while also making influential friends. In every town, the most important business people, civic leaders, and politicians will be members of service clubs.

Take care to join for all the right reasons, and be prepared to shell out some of your time and treasure. Members of service clubs can quickly spot someone trying only to "net-work" without really wanting to work. Such working together, by the way, creates the best relationships.

In *The Four Loves,* C. S. Lewis wrote something that really offended me when I first read it. Lewis said that friendship has to be "about something" other than just the two friends. [45] In my teenaged idealism, I thought friendship should be *only* about the two friends. The idea that a friendship needed a third "something" in order to last seemed jaded to me. But I soon learned the wisdom of Lewis's observation. Friendships need a common interest, a project, in order to last. Even marital friendships need a project. The friendships forged at church in service to the Great Commission, as well as those built in secular service clubs, can be extremely satisfying and can last because of the value added by the shared project.

Fundraising dinners and other events can provide another excellent venue for meeting leaders and visionary people. Nonprofit organizations work hard to get the most visionary, generous, and influential people to attend their banquets, and you can't find a better place to meet movers and shakers. If you attend a fundraising dinner, be ready to make a contribution that will cover the cost of your attendance and meal. Usually, $100 will cover it all. The ethical rule is to "do no harm" by attending. Your presence will encourage the people who have sponsored the event (since larger attendance always feels more encouraging than slight attendance), your gift will help pay for the event, and you may feel prompted to give an additional amount or to find a way to volunteer for the organization. Everyone wins. In the meantime, you get an excellent opportunity to meet interesting people.

> **"**
> **FRIENDSHIPS NEED A COMMON INTEREST, A PROJECT, IN ORDER TO LAST.**
> **"**

Party politics, the Chamber of Commerce, professional associations, neighborhood associations, and any other activity that brings people together can give you other opportunities to build your network and bring kingdom values to bear on the work of the world. In the best cases, you may get to introduce new friends into the kingdom by putting them in touch with the King.

THE IMPORTANCE OF DIVERSITY

Make sure that you include people of the opposite gender in your network. Women are quickly establishing themselves as a majority among managers in the workforce. According to Hanna Rosin,

> Women now earn 60 percent of master's degrees, about half of all law and medical degrees, and 42 percent of all M.B.A.s. Most important, women earn almost 60 percent of all bachelor's degrees—the minimum requirement, in most cases, for an affluent life. [46]

The idea of a business or any profession operating as "an old boys' club" is becoming increasingly absurd. Men who cut themselves off from networking with women set themselves up for failure. Women have long understood the need to network with men if they want to prosper professionally.

Some Christian men fail to network with women out of fear that some women will misinterpret their overtures as a desire to cultivate a romantic connection. Among ministers, the so-called Billy Graham Rule has often held sway, by which male ministers avoided ever being alone with a woman. Accordingly, many ministers still refuse to have coffee with a woman, much less lunch. Sometimes ministry teams leave women out of retreats and other

> **"**
> **MEN WHO CUT THEMSELVES OFF FROM NETWORKING WITH WOMEN SET THEMSELVES UP FOR FAILURE.**
> **"**

bonding events in order to observe a vague corollary of the Graham Rule. [47] While following the Billy Graham Rule gives an iron-clad guarantee that a man will not commit adultery with a woman, it can also serve as a tool of male dominance. If a man chooses to adopt it (as I confess that I long ago did), he must make an extra effort to ensure that he is neither shutting women out of his network nor out of his circle of power.

Consider just a few ideas—certainly not the final word—that may help to mitigate the negative effects of the Billy Graham Rule:

- Meeting a person of the opposite gender in a public place doesn't constitute "being alone." Understand, however, that acting in public in an inappropriate way that *appears* romantic is unprofessional and will set people talking in ways that will hurt you. In business settings, old Southerners like me may want to cut back on some of the gallantries we learned as children. Some unwittingly use them as a tool of dominance, and they can create sexual misunderstandings.
- Meeting in an office doesn't constitute "being alone" if you leave the door open or if the office has an adequate "transparency window" that gives nearby people visual access to the room. If you have authority in your workplace, never allow office doors in your area to lack transparency windows, nor allow employees to block the office-door window with paper or other opaque materials. Offices are not private spaces.

- Gender-exclusive staff retreats, such as golf outings for male staff, are usually inappropriate. If you have only one woman on your staff, and if you have more than just a few staff members, you may be discriminating against women.
- At receptions, force yourself to engage first with a person of the opposite gender. This habit will keep you from automatically favoring people of your gender.
- Look through your Facebook or LinkedIn lists and count how many of your friends and contacts are of the opposite gender. If you see great lopsidedness in one direction or the other, start making more friends of the opposite gender. As you begin that effort, you may want to talk to your spouse (if you have one) and explain what you are doing and why.
- If you sense sexual tension in a professional relationship with a person of the opposite gender, get yourself under control. You should never punish someone else just because you are psychologically immature. [48] In such cases, you may need to see a counselor for assistance, which likely will uncover other problems that you've tried to ignore.

These guidelines won't work for everyone, and you must decide for yourself what works for you. Married people should decide their policy in dialogue with their spouses. Not everyone handles romantic feelings in a mature way, and people under stress can go backwards in that area of maturity. You can't ignore the issue

> **GOD IS BUILDING THE KINGDOM FOR *EVERY* NATION, PEOPLE, TONGUE, AND TRIBE, SO KINGDOM NETWORKING SHOULD REFLECT THAT DIVERSITY.**

of sexual temptation; it costs too much. If you struggle with it, get spiritual or psychological counseling. The more justice you can achieve in this matter, the stronger your networks will become.

When we consider human diversity, we ought to include *multiple* categories of diversity, such as race, ethnicity, economic status, personality type, and others. God is building the kingdom for *every* nation, people, tongue, and tribe, so kingdom networking should reflect that diversity. Including people unlike yourself, not only benefits people who have traditionally been excluded, it ensures that you don't cut yourself off from the benefits of having a wide and diverse personal network.

Consider a few helpful principles as you connect with new people. While they certainly don't exhaust the topic, they may help you to develop a set of tools that fits your talents and circumstances.

ACQUIRE ADEQUATE NETWORKING STATIONERY

Consider proper business stationery your first tool for effective networking. This includes (1) business cards that minimally include your name, phone number, and email address. Some people have cards with just their name on them so they can make a point of specially writing down their phone number or email address for those they deem worthy, but I have always seen that practice as a bit pretentious; (2) all-purpose, personalized note cards (not the

3 X 5 or 4 X 6 index cards you use for making notes, but rather the folded kind you use for thank-you notes and the like); (3) business/professional letterhead for writing serious business letters.

The linchpin for networkers is the business card. Never, *ever* go anywhere without a supply of them. You never know when you'll meet someone important to you (and to whom you may become important). The business card provides a durable record of the people you've met and often provides a contextual clue for where you met them. Without cards, you could lose most of your new contacts. Keep your cards in all your jackets, a few in your wallet or purse, in your car, in your mobile phone case, in your briefcase, and anywhere else you can think of. Don't go anywhere without them!

At the same time, understand that others may not carry their cards so religiously. I wrote the previous paragraph some time ago, and since then I have taken to sending my electronic card by text message or email. I greatly prefer that others send me their contact information in the same way, as it saves me time in transcribing their information to my cell phone and helps me avoid errors in transcription. While I can send my card quickly that way, some people have yet to master their cell phone. Whatever you do, don't tease people about the way they want to give you their contact information!

Anything beats relying on your memory alone. You can't avoid having to depend on your memory for some things, but if you're anything like me, take steps to avoid such a precarious fate when getting contact data. Asking for a person's business card provides the smoothest way of getting the contact information you need that will enable you to follow up later. Having to write your data on a scrap of paper looks more than a little amateurish.

No matter how gregarious and friendly you may be, it can feel daunting to introduce yourself to people you don't know and to begin a conversation with them. On personality tests, I score as an extreme extrovert. But I will confess that sometimes, I'm just not up to interacting with others. I see a crowd of new people, and I just want to run away. Sometimes, I don't want to be around people. So even though I'm pretty good at meeting people, I understand the fears or reluctance you may have about it. Still, kingdom work requires that you meet people.

Imagine that you're at a reception, perhaps an office party or a conference, or just standing around, waiting to get into a church or a theatre. Making the most of such wide-open opportunities is a key networking skill. So, get ready to take advantage of it.

> **"**
> **KINGDOM WORK REQUIRES THAT YOU MEET PEOPLE.**
> **"**

Before you try to meet new people, let me introduce you to yourself. (Yes, you read that right.) Write down the six things that most interest you, or the six things you know the best. Those six things are your fishhooks. You will use them to engage people in what some might mistakenly call "small talk." True small talk refers to standing or sitting around and just running your mouth about things you don't really care about to people who have no interest in the conversation. It can serve a good function as "space filler," but most people don't do it well, and even if it feels better than silence, no one sheds any tears when it ends.

Avoid small talk by speaking of things that really interest you. If you're attending a conference, probably the topic of the conference interests nearly everyone there, so it may provide a good topic for discussion. But let's say you don't know the common interest, but you know you like sports, politics, religion, food, travel, and technology. Almost everyone has an interest in at least one of those topics. Finding something mutually interesting to talk about provides a great way to start a relationship. So introduce yourself and start asking questions. Even taciturn people do better either asking or answering questions than they do just trying to come up with something spontaneous to talk about.

Just a few questions should help you figure out what common interests you have with nearly anyone. (A bit later I'll give you a list of some good ones.) I love the old Latin quote from the ancient comedian Terentius (185–159 BC): *"Homo sum: humani nihil a me alienum puto."* It means, "I am a man: nothing human do I consider strange." [49] We share a basic humanness with every other human being in the world, so we have something in common with everyone. As a comedian, Terentius depended on that truth in order to make people laugh. I like the Spanish existentialist philosopher Miguel de Unamuno's version of the quote even better: *"Homo sum: nullum hominem a me alienum puto."* [50] In English, it means, "I am a man, and I consider no other man strange." Unamuno had far more interest in particular flesh-and-bone human beings than in abstract humanity.

I like the quote in both cases, but I think I heard the best version in college from my friend, Russell Steen: "You're weird, Joe, but it's okay. Everybody is weird." Although Russell Steen and Unamuno say exactly opposite things ("no one is weird" vs.

"everyone is weird"), they essentially agree. If everyone is weird, then no one is weird. We are all in this human thing together. So, you might look at meeting and getting to know people as an exercise in figuring out in what ways both you and the other person share weirdness. If you worry about seeming weird, you have it all wrong. Being weird is a problem only if you're alone. Being weird together with another weird person is called *fellowship*, and you can pretty quickly cover the distance between fellowship and friendship.

Effective networking means you must learn to "read" people. We might call this the Sherlock Holmes principle. If you've read any of Arthur Conan Doyle's stories or seen movies or plays about this great detective, then you know how he would deduce the details of someone's life by making observations about the individual's appearance. That's a lot easier to do in fiction than it is in person! Nevertheless, good networkers learn to observe people and, if they can't deduce their story, at least they can discern their disposition.

I like to say that I've found the key to understanding women. Such a declaration always gets people's attention, especially men, because none of them believe me and they want to see me make a fool of myself. As they wait for the punch line of a witty joke, I then reveal the secret: *The key to understanding women is to understand that they are all different.* Each one of them is an individual to herself, and no general rule will "explain" every woman. My rule explains each of them, not all of them; and there's a big difference between "each" of them and "all" of them. I always tell men that if they want to understand their wives, they're going to have to pay attention to them!

The same truth applies to men. *Everybody* is different—and the key to effective people work is to pay attention to them. Whether you find yourself in a room full of people you don't know or seated at a table with new people, you won't know the right thing to say unless you tune into the people you want to engage. Do they seem involved or interested in the meeting? Do they seem distanced? Do they look tired? Do they look sad? Do they seem uncomfortable? Are they young or old, male or female, local or cosmopolitan, native-born or foreigners? What can you

> **IF EVERYONE IS WEIRD, THEN NO ONE IS WEIRD. WE ARE ALL IN THIS HUMAN THING TOGETHER.**

tell about them from the way they dress? That includes not only *what* they wear, but *how* they wear it. If you don't pay attention to that little detail, you may not realize that you're trying to network the waiters. Now, you may *want* to do exactly that, as I often do. You want to keep the staff on your side, and treating them with courtesy and taking them seriously can endear you to them, so long as you don't get in the way of their work.

Don't miss the main point here: Size folks up before you open your big mouth and start yapping. But do it fast! Nobody likes being stared at; that's just creepy. Paying attention, however, isn't creepy—it's the height of courtesy. Once you have formed a working hypothesis about someone you intend to speak to, the "game" becomes pretty simple.

Once you have sized up your situation, consider two easy steps to starting a new connection. First, step up and introduce yourself and your association: "I'm Joe Castleberry from Northwest University." A person who doesn't perceive you as a threat will usually offer you their name, though it may surprise you how many people do not. If they fail to tell you their name, it doesn't mean they don't want to meet you. Some people just have an inadequate grasp of the rules of courtesy. Lamentably, I sometimes fail to capture a person's name at the beginning of a conversation. If you do the same, go ahead and pursue the conversation; don't worry about their name. Later on, you can ask for it directly, or you can offer your business card and request theirs. If they give you their card, then you have a reminder of their name. *Don't stuff it immediately in your pocket,* but rather, take a moment to glance over it appreciatively. If they don't have a card, go ahead and give them yours. [51]

Second, after the networking partner has responded to your greeting, you may want to begin the conversation with a question. Appropriate questions serve as a polite and effective way to get to know people. Remember that the *primary* purpose of your efforts isn't for the other person to get to know you, but rather, for you to learn about them. If you don't know who they are, you won't be able to effectively serve them, and service is the *essence of kingdom activity.* (Never forget that "service" and "ministry" are translated from a single Greek word, *diakonia*, in the New Testament.) Everyone inside the kingdom is a minister; ministry is our sacred life calling, to people both outside and inside the kingdom. Like everything else in the kingdom, networking is not about you and your needs. But if you network faithfully, God will richly meet your needs.

> **IF YOU NETWORK FAITHFULLY, GOD WILL RICHLY MEET YOUR NEEDS.**

You can ask many kinds of questions, but remember that the purpose of your questioning is to figure out what kind of "big talk" (as opposed to "small talk") you should draw out of your new friend. Engage the other person in conversation so you can figure out what kind of shared big-talk interests you have. That big talk will allow you to begin a personal relationship, not just a business relationship. So should you begin with business talk or personal talk? You will have to decide that through your reading of that person. If people seem eager and open, you can go straight to business talk and then work the personal stuff in to increase your likeability. If the person seems disengaged, you may want to take the personal route first.

GOOD QUESTIONS TO ASK

Good questions come in all shapes and sizes. Consider just a few categories of effective conversation-starting questions:

1. *Enjoyment question:* Are you enjoying the conference/convention/event?
2. *Source question:* Where do you work? What do you do there?
3. *Interest question:* Which speakers/topics have you found the most interesting?
4. *Experience question:* How long have you been in this industry/profession/line of work?
5. *Escape question:* Did you hear the jazz band playing in the other hall? (Or did you notice the football game playing on the big-screen TV in the lobby, or some other thing going on in the area that you noticed and think they might be interested in).

6. *Commiseration question:* I just hate these kinds of events, don't you? (Don't say it if you don't mean it.)

7. *At-ease question:* I'm totally lost here. Do you know what's going on? (If they're lost, they've found a partner. If they're not, they can feel good about lending you a helping hand.)

8. *Who-do-you-know question:* Oh, you're from X! Do you know Bob Smith? (It's best not to ask about the most prominent person in their company, organization, or hometown.)

9. *Origin question:* Where are you from?

All these questions encourage people to talk about the event or about themselves. By engaging their minds in this way, you learn how you might serve them. That service may involve getting them to participate in your business or vision. The fact that they are helping you doesn't mean you aren't helping them. The kingdom net is always a multi-directional flow of information, service, and blessing.

Whatever questions you use, tailor them to the situation and the person. You'll get better at it the more you practice the craft.

After you ask a question, respond with a little personal information before moving to the follow-up question. But keep your own talking to a minimum. People don't want to feel impressed with you; they want you to feel impressed with them. Don't disappoint them! Express real interest in what they say. As they realize that you find them interesting, they'll want to know more about you. No one attracts people more than the person who takes a sincere interest in them.

These rules generally apply whether you're attending a conference, being friendly on the train, visiting a park or a church or any other venue where people meet. Ask people questions, and as you find out more information about them, it will reveal to you exactly how they are special (read: weird) and what interests you share. Anne of Green Gables called

> **"NO ONE ATTRACTS PEOPLE MORE THAN THE PERSON WHO TAKES A SINCERE INTEREST IN THEM."**

people with common interests her "kindred spirits." [52] Once you figure out that *all* human beings are your kin, you will realize that the world is full of kindred spirits.

INTERNET SOCIAL NETWORKING

People have differing ideas about the use of social networking tools such as Facebook, Twitter, and LinkedIn. I'm partial to Facebook. Some people keep a tight rein on their accounts, allowing only close friends or well-known associates into their network. So far, I've found no benefit in restricting access to my "friends." I use a couple of filters to deny a few "friend invitations," one of which is "pornography-aversion." If anyone sends me a friend invitation that has a racy picture, I deny the request. Too many folk are out there trolling for customers, and I don't wish to receive their notes. In general, however, I find it useful to accept almost any friend who offers their electronic hand. As a result, I have collected almost 5,000 "likes."

When I hit the limit of 5,000, I turned the profile into a business page and began to rebuild my personal profile. I use Facebook for both personal and business purposes. (If you hit that limit and don't want to open a business page, you can always go through your list and discreetly de-friend 100 people you don't know and with whom you never correspond. All files of any kind require maintenance and purging.) If you do convert to a business page, maintain a personal profile for your closest friends. Through both my personal and business sites, I have made some dandy contacts on Internet social media that have brought business and kingdom yields.

Using social media provides wonderful benefits. Whenever I make a new contact, soon afterward I search for the person on Facebook, and if I find him or her, I send a friend request right away. This practice can reap a number of benefits:

1. you gain access to their contact data;
2. they get an instant reminder of your meeting that helps them remember who you are;
3. you get a regular reminder of who they are, as their posts get reported back to you;
4. they get a reminder of who you are in the same way;
5. you get updates on their activities—sometimes even a heads-up that they will be in the same place as you;
6. you have a clear path to maintaining future communications.

Facebook is truly an outstanding professional tool for maintaining personal networks, whether through minimal or constant contact.

I should probably tell you that with almost 5,000 Facebook connections, I don't spend a lot of time poring over everyone's status updates. I rarely spend more than fifteen minutes a day on Facebook, and I don't always do it at the same time of day. I try to update my status every day, which regularly keeps my name and comments in front of my friends, and I'll make a few comments on other people's status if I find their comments amusing or otherwise noteworthy. I read the personal messages that people have sent me, and I clean up the

> **" FACEBOOK IS TRULY AN OUTSTANDING PROFESSIONAL TOOL FOR MAINTAINING PERSONAL NETWORKS. "**

mass mailings that inevitably get sent around. I assiduously avoid the extra features and games, for which I have no time or use.

In truth, I don't read a lot of status updates. I do read a random sampling of the hundreds or even thousands of updates that pop up. But even that random sampling brings people to my mind and allows me to make intentional contact with various individuals. Since the people on my Facebook page come from every period of my life, I find such sampling rewarding and satisfying.

FRIENDING NEW CONTACTS ON SOCIAL MEDIA

In professional life, we often find that we need to meet a certain person but have no obvious or immediate natural path to such a meeting. In looking through the contacts of a new friend, I once saw the name of an important person I had hoped to meet for some time. I immediately sent that eminent person a friend request, stating relevant data as follows:

Greeting: Hi, Mr. Jones.

Identity and Role: I'm Joseph Castleberry, President of Northwest University.

Reputation: I have heard of you often in recent months and have been impressed by what I have seen and heard of your work.

(Truthful) Network Links: My friend Jerry McIntosh, has spoken highly of you and suggested that we should meet.

Expression of Privilege: I would count it a real privilege to meet you in person as (the Lord/opportunity) permits.

Suggestion of Utility: I have some ideas about how we may be able to collaborate on matters of mutual interest.

Invitation to Association: I hope you'll accept me as a Facebook friend in the meantime, and that we'll soon meet face to face.

Would you believe, the very next day I visited a church hosting a prominent guest speaker, and it "just so happened" that "Mr. Jones" was present. After the service, as I stood around in the vestibule of the church, he walked up to me and introduced himself, thanked me for the Facebook note, and we have been friends ever since. It turned out that he knew who I was and also had been looking forward to meeting me. Several of our friends had mentioned that we should meet—but it's a long way from hearing such comments to actually seeing them happen.

Serious networkers don't wait around for fate to smile on them. They take fate by the arm and gently, politely, take charge of its direction. People who "just happen" to get lucky and make good contacts are not networkers. They may be caught up in the net, but they are hardly fishers of people. They're just fish. Networkers take up the net and use it to go fishing. It may

> **SERIOUS NETWORKERS DON'T WAIT AROUND FOR FATE TO SMILE ON THEM. THEY TAKE FATE BY THE ARM AND GENTLY, POLITELY, TAKE CHARGE OF ITS DIRECTION.**

feel a little fishy to some to actively (and even aggressively) network, but as the gangster character Hyman Roth famously said of a polar opposite kind of activity in *The Godfather: Part II,* "This is the business we've chosen." [53] If you're a part of the kingdom of God, then you must take up the people net and work it for God's purposes.

WHEN FRIENDSHIP BREAKS OUT

Working together with people on a great project creates the best relationships. Sometimes, those relationships become important friendships. Not every relationship becomes a friendship, and frankly, sometimes it's hard to recognize the difference between the two.

We might arrange relationships on an "intensity continuum" between a casual meeting in which we forget names (not much of a relationship at all) to being identical twins (an intense relationship) or marrying your best friend. I imagine that a mother could feel even more intensely related to her child than twins feel to each other, or that I feel to my best-friend wife (but I'm only guessing). At any rate, it's an intensely personal decision to determine where a relationship becomes a friendship. We might say that a friendship is worth more than a mere relationship, but even that depends on how you measure worth.

Every human has inestimable worth, so we can never say that any relationship lacks value. Still, not every relationship has the same worth or importance. Strangely enough, a casual relationship could outweigh the most personal relationship . . . in certain circumstances. If you have just suffered a terrible automobile accident, your relationship to the emergency medical technician who is saving your life is, at least for the moment, more important than any other relationship you have. Never devalue *any* relationship and treat someone as if he or she were not important. In the right situation, any relationship might become the most important one in your life.

> **"**
> **IN THE RIGHT SITUATION, ANY RELATIONSHIP MIGHT BECOME THE MOST IMPORTANT ONE IN YOUR LIFE.**
> **"**

Friendship has many levels. Your closest friends might be the ones you would call if you had only an hour to live and could make only five or ten phone calls. Some people consider a relationship to be a friendship only if they think they can share their deepest thoughts and feelings with the other person. You might think a lot of people fit that definition, or you might count only a handful of friends. The difference comes down to personality.

Dunbar's number theorizes that people can maintain stable social relationships only with a community of around 150 people. In such a social system, each of the people knows all of the other people and how they relate to each other. [54] That doesn't mean you can't have more than 150 friends, but rather that you can have a true community of only about that number. But friendship includes many other kinds of relationships. I don't restrict it to those in my closest group or to those with whom I can share my deepest feelings. I call *hundreds* of people my friends because they consistently treat me with goodwill. That may seem like a pretty low bar for defining friendship, but it works for me. Other people might be called "friendly acquaintances." Such people act in a friendly way toward you, but you don't know them well enough to discern whether they would act in a consistently friendly way if it were not in their immediate interests to do so. Some acquaintances have no particular feeling toward you. Finally, enemies don't like you and actively work against you.

The following table contrasts friends and friendly acquaintances:

Friends	Friendly Acquaintances
Will phone you to talk about their deepest thoughts and feelings.	Will accept a phone call from you if you're paying for it.
Can be trusted to watch your back.	Will watch your back if they're behind you and are going in the same direction.

Would visit you in the hospital if you were sick.	Would visit you in the hospital if they had something to gain from it.
Enjoys collaborating with you in a cause or project.	Needs your help in a cause or project.
Calls just to see how you are doing.	Calls just when they need you to do something.
Celebrates your victories.	Celebrates when you win together on the same team.

While there's nothing wrong with being merely a friendly acquaintance, a friendly acquaintance is not as dear as a friend. The lines do not remain static, either. A friendly acquaintance today may become a close friend at just the right time. So the more friendly acquaintances you make, the more potential friends you have. When friendly acquaintances join together in the cause of the kingdom, and when the Holy Spirit fuses a strong bond between them, amazing blessings can result.

WORKING THE NET

1. If you don't have adequate professional stationery, order it now. Be sure to include your best phone number, email address, and social media contacts, as well as your organizational association and job title. If you serve as a board member of a nonprofit organization, you may want to ask for cards from that organization that identify you as such. It may help you as you engage in fundraising and "friend-raising" for the organization.

2. If you haven't signed up for Facebook or LinkedIn or another social media platform, go online now and do so. You have a lot of fun waiting as you start catching up with people you have known over the years! If you want to "friend" someone who knows you, send a simple friend invitation. If you want to connect with someone you haven't met, use the format provided in this chapter. For serious networkers, I recommend building a large social media portfolio.

3. Make plans to attend a professional development conference or a ministry conference as soon as possible. Set a goal of establishing three to five new connections through friendly conversations with people who share your profession or interest. If needed, use the outline of questions provided in this chapter to strike up conversations. Follow up on at least one of the connections with a concrete action proposal.

CHAPTER FOUR

THINK

THE MISSION OF GOD AND THE HUMAN MISSION

C hi-Dooh "Skip" Li founded his legal practice in 1977 with the vision of building "a law firm with a conscience." Considered by his peers to be one of the super-lawyers of the Pacific Northwest, he's a truly committed Christian. All of the lawyers at his firm care deeply about their clients, their community, and the entire human race. Each of them gets the job done for their clients in the right way.

If Skip did nothing but practice law, he would still have deserved mention in this book. As a consummate Christian professional, his work constitutes real ministry and a real expression of the kingdom of God in his life, spreading God's reign into the lives and businesses of the people he represents. As he obeys the Holy Spirit's direction in serving them, he powerfully influences them to live out kingdom principles and fulfill the will of God. How could it get better than that?

But it does get better!

Back in 1982, before his law firm was fully five years old and before his considerable reputation had matured in Seattle, he heard the famous Argentinian preacher Juan Carlos Ortiz speak at his home church. Ortiz pointed out that President Reagan had just announced $300 million in military support for Central American countries to fight off communism. "With that kind of money," Ortiz said parenthetically, "you could buy all the land in Central America and give it to the poor, and then you wouldn't have to fight the Communists." [55] Ortiz' "parenthesis" became Skip's clarion call from God.

Skip had an intimate sense of the needs of the poor, landless *campesinos* of Central America. Born in India as the son of Chinese diplomats, Skip had spent the formative years of his youth in Central America, mastering the Spanish language and coming to a deep and personal understanding of the social and economic deprivation of its poorest people. He knew that the most vulnerable individuals had no land of their own. Their meager livelihood depended on others hiring them at skin-and-bone wages. As God began to give him a vision, he tried to find other people to lead an effort to buy land for the poor. As others declined to take the lead, he came to understand that God was calling him to help poor people buy their own farmland and build new communities and villages to support themselves economically.

Skip knew he had limited time and resources, and he also knew that God had not called him to move to Central America to spend his whole attention on building a rural development agency. So he began to use his growing personal network to raise funds and marshal expertise into his new vision, which he called Agros International.

At this writing, Agros has established forty-two villages in rural areas of Guatemala, El Salvador, Nicaragua, Honduras, and Mexico. Not only did Agros buy the land and help the people settle on it (developing a better society than they had ever known), it did so in a way that preserved and established the dignity of the people. Rather than give them the land, Agros extended credit to help them *buy* individual plots. They have successfully begun to repay their land loans, and many now possess clear title to their land. In all of the villages, families who had suffered extreme poverty for generations have established a whole new dignified life in which they can flourish in the mission of God.

A few months ago, I attended a fundraising banquet in Seattle to hear more about Skip's work. Hundreds of people came out, and I saw nodes and connections everywhere. Some of the attendees were successful new landowners who had come from half a world away to tell their story of success. Others had worked directly with the new landowners, teaching them principles of development and self-sufficiency, helping them build clean water systems, and providing for community health needs and education for the children. Others had helped set up rural banking institutions. Still others had done nothing more than contribute financially. Many had traveled to Central America to see the work. All together, they have formed a powerful network that, in the name of Jesus and in obedience to God's reign, is breaking the intergenerational cycle of poverty with a holistic, sustainable, long-term strategy for development and prosperity.

I had spent too much time among the poor of Central and South America to ignore their plight, especially when faced with a proven, successful expression of the kingdom. So I sensed the Holy Spirit's direction and wove myself right into the network. I wrote a check. I look forward to seeing in what other ways I might contribute to this amazing network. (You can get involved at www.agros.org.)

THE MISSION OF GOD

Skip Li and his partners in the Agros network don't call themselves missionaries, but they carry out the mission of God. Unfortunately, most people have a very limited concept of the mission of God, but networkers who follow Jesus *must* come to understand it.

> **THE NETWORK OF GOD'S MISSION GOES BEYOND THE TRINITY.**

Throughout most of church history, the term *mission* was unknown. Before the Protestant Reformation, the term *mission* always referred to God's own mission, what theologians called the *Missio Dei* (Latin for "mission of God"). They placed the emphasis on God's own sending within the Trinity. The Father and the Spirit send the Son; the Father and Son send the Spirit; the Father, Son and Spirit send the church. The Trinity itself was the first missional network.

But the network of God's mission goes beyond the Trinity.

The mission of God consists of three integrated parts. The first part is the Trinitarian mission, rooted in the very nature of a missionary God. The first chapter of Genesis suggests that the mutual sending of the members of the Trinity accomplished creation itself. The Father sent forth the Word to create the world, and the Holy Spirit moved over the chaos, like the finger of God, to bring order to it all. All of God's missional work in the world is Trinitarian, involving every part of God's being.

THE MISSION OF HUMANITY

The second part of God's mission is the mission of humanity, or *missio humanitatis*. Genesis 1:28 prescribes the mission of humanity; but before we look at that verse, let's review the process of creation.

The creative power of the Word of God informs the whole story of creation. At the beginning of the story, God spoke the formless and empty world into existence. Then God declared, "Let there be light," and immediately, light appeared. A declaration of the division of the waters followed, then the division of water and dry land, and then the sprouting of seed-bearing plants. Each time God declared the emergence of a new aspect of creation, it occurred. We see no struggle or resistance. God's Word overpowered the emptiness.

God went on to declare the creation of the living creatures of the sea and the birds and beasts of the air and land. Every time God spoke, the Word prevailed. And then, as the crowning act of creation, God declared the making of humanity in the divine image and likeness. Up until that point, the Hebrew text of Genesis clips along in elegant but sober prose. But when creation reaches its zenith, prose no longer suffices. Just as in an old-fashioned musical drama, the story bursts into song as soon as humans appear. "So God created mankind in his own image" the song begins. "In the image of God he created them," the song lilts as it repeats the strain, but in reverse order. "Male and female he created them," it concludes, setting the scene for God's first declaration of blessing upon humanity. [56]

We see clearly the dramatic nature of God's first declaration of blessing. Nothing could more plainly indicate God's good pleasure toward us. While the text celebrates the earliest aspects of the creation with the refrain, "and God saw that it was good," the emergence of the higher animals and humanity call for a blessing from God. As for the animals, God blesses them with the command to be fruitful and multiply, to fill the seas and the water and the air. But in blessing humans, God adds a dimension not included in the blessing of the animals.

Look at the first blessing God pronounces on humanity:

God blessed them and said to them, "Be fruitful and increase in number; fill the earth and subdue it. Rule over the fish of the sea and the birds in the sky and over every living creature that moves on the ground." [57]

Notice that the blessing includes a set of commands. When God wants to bless us, He usually tells us what to do. That's why we might appropriately call the Ten Commandments the Ten Blessings. People who keep the commands of God bring great blessing on themselves. God doesn't command us merely to control us, but rather to point us toward maximum blessings. Imagine a host who prepared a great banquet for his guests, but they never got to eat it because he never told them about it, never invited them to sit down and eat. God doesn't treat us like that but, rather, gives us commands that ensure maximum blessing.

THE TRIPLE MANDATE

The first blessing includes a set of three commands: multiply, migrate, and rule. These three commands make up the human mission, and each of them requires humans to interact and cooperate with each other and with God.

MULTIPLY

The essence of God's blessing involves a mission that brings the fullest degree of cooperation to human life. The first command—to *multiply*, to be fruitful and increase in number—essentially called on men and women to love one another. By committing to one another in love, human beings would bring on themselves one of God's greatest blessings, children.

MIGRATE

Obviously, the human mission doesn't end with reproduction and children. It goes on to command human beings to "fill the earth."

> **GOD DOESN'T COMMAND US MERELY TO CONTROL US, BUT RATHER TO POINT US TOWARD MAXIMUM BLESSINGS.**

Filling the earth implies *migration*—and human beings have become the most fully distributed species on earth. We've found a way to spread to every corner of the earth. We live in rain forests and deserts, frozen poles and tropical islands, mountain heights and the lowest valleys. We've conquered the seas, the land, and the air, using them as the lanes of our migration. We've even visited the moon, and we may someday figure out how to live there! In all of these endeavors, humans have to work together and establish networks to survive.

As we have moved throughout the earth, we have fulfilled an important aspect of God's plan. We have become spectacularly diverse. We see the importance of that fact for God's mission in Revelation 7:9–10, where we note the endgame of God's mission on earth:

> After this I looked, and there before me was a great multitude that no one could count, from every nation, tribe, people and language, standing before the throne and before the Lamb. They were wearing white robes and were holding palm branches in their hands. And they cried out in a loud voice: "Salvation belongs to our God, who sits on the throne, and to the Lamb."

Notice that as John beheld the fruit of God's mission—the gathering of all those redeemed in Christ—he recognized men and women from every nation, people, tongue, and tribe.

How did John know they came from every human group? He could see their differences. He could see the different skin tones and facial characteristics, and he could hear their different languages. He couldn't see any national costumes, since they all wore white robes, but their diversity remained intact, even in eternity. In one sense, they were all the same. The same thing had saved them all: the blood of the Lamb. It had equally cleansed them all of their sins, as symbolized by their white robes. But their ethnic and language diversity remained intact.

By commanding humanity to fill the earth, God made sure that people would *not* stay the same. As some traveled north, they grew whiter. As others moved toward the Equator, they grew darker. As they separated from each other, their languages diverged from one another. (When the people at Babel refused to scatter and tried to draw all humanity back together, God turbo-charged the diversity process by confusing their languages. But languages have changed naturally ever since. Today's Spanish, Portuguese, French, Italian, and Romanian all used to be simple Latin, until it rubbed up against the local languages of the Roman Empire. If you've ever read Beowulf, you know how much English has changed in just a thousand years.) [58]

> **"**
> **AS WE HAVE MOVED THROUGHOUT THE EARTH, WE HAVE FULFILLED AN IMPORTANT ASPECT OF GOD'S PLAN. WE HAVE BECOME SPECTACULARLY DIVERSE.**
> **"**

As people mixed together after migrating, and then re-migrating, more and more diversity resulted. All of this made the heart of God glad. God loves diversity and the primordial, divine plan gave humanity a mission that would result in great ethnic diversity. And so God planned for childbirth and families to bring about billions of human beings, and for migration to make us different from each other. We share these characteristics with the animals, as God also commanded the animals to be fruitful and fill the earth. But the third unique command, God gave only to human beings. It represents our greatest distinction from the rest of creation.

"Subdue [the earth]. Rule over the fish of the sea and the birds in the sky and over every living creature that moves on the ground." [59] In this command, God gave humanity an incredible responsibility and privilege. While remaining Sovereign over creation, God would rule on earth *through* human beings. (Jesus didn't introduce the kingdom of God concept. We see it throughout the Old Testament, from Genesis to Malachi.)

> **GOD LOVES DIVERSITY AND THE PRIMORDIAL, DIVINE PLAN GAVE HUMANITY A MISSION THAT WOULD RESULT IN GREAT ETHNIC DIVERSITY.**

Theologians from the Reformed tradition have often called this third command in the first blessing "the dominion mandate." God didn't want human beings to sit around, exposed to the elements and the hunger of wild animals. Neither did God intend for us to remain hunters and gatherers forever. God's plan called for human beings to establish their rule over the earth, including its elements and its animals. This involved agriculture and hunting, building homes and sewing garments.

Some might object that all of these elements resulted from the fall of mankind, but cold and heat didn't come from the fall. The fruits of agriculture and the husbandry of animals didn't arise from the fall. They all formed part of God's plan for blessing humanity from the beginning. While the fall changed the way we experience cold and heat and rain and agriculture and other cultural factors of human life and society, these elements of human life would have existed with or without the fall.

In any event, God knew before the creation of the world that the fall would occur. Knowing that human free will would eventually open the door to sin, God planned the redemption of a multiethnic, multilingual, multicultural, globally scattered human race from the very beginning. God's mission in the world is neither an afterthought nor a result of the fall.

The scattering of humanity, part of the human mission, resulted in more than varied skin tones and languages. God's command for us to subdue the earth and rule it also implied cultural differences. Nancy Pearcey has explained that "subdue the earth" means to harness the natural world: plant crops, build bridges, design computers, compose music. This passage is sometimes called the Cultural Mandate because it tells us that our original purpose was to create cultures, build civilizations—nothing less. [60]

As human beings build homes and villages and cities, they also invent ways of living in them. Anyone who has ever left his or her hometown knows that culture varies from place to place. Far from being a curse, different cultures represent an amazing blessing. Today I took a Mexican friend to an Indian restaurant so he could sample one of the world's great cuisines. It truly amazes me how a plate of chicken can look and taste so different from place to place around the world. Southern-fried, wrapped in an enchilada, baked in a tandouri, sautéed in a wok, or skewered in a shish kebab, chicken itself doesn't always taste like chicken. In today's world-class cities, we live in the multicolored splendor of fully-grown, global human gardens, flush with the full flowering of God's plan for a gloriously diverse human race.

IS HUMANITY A FAILURE?

We celebrate cultural diversity today more vigorously than at any other time in human history. The horrors of World War II and the Holocaust caused most of the world to see the wickedness of hating anyone because of cultural, racial, or personal differences. As a result, colonialism fell apart. The Civil Rights Movement flourished in America. The peoples of the world began to hope for democracy and prosperity. The richest nations on earth launched a program of development that has transformed much of the world. The conditions of human life on our planet have never been better in recorded history.

> **THE HUMAN MISSION WILL SUCCEED, DESPITE THE FAILINGS OF HUMANITY.**

And God's great enterprise rolls on.

The fall indeed caused a great deal of damage to the human mission, but God hasn't failed. The human mission will succeed, despite the failings of humanity. Because of the cross of Jesus Christ, a great multitude that no one can number will gather to celebrate God's victory in creating, saving, and redeeming humanity. The mission will succeed as the kingdom net makes the salvation of God known.

Our work is not in vain.

WORKING THE NET

God focused on three commands in declaring the human mission statement: multiply, migrate, and rule. All are crucial to kingdom networking. Consider the following ideas:

1. Family life is mission. How does your family help you carry out the mission to which God has called you? Beyond the obvious fact of reproducing the human population, how are children important in making God's mission flourish? If you have children, raising them is a crucial element of your calling in the kingdom net. How do your children open up networking connections for you?

2. Travel is the mother's milk of the modern economy. Opportunities to travel or to move to a new area open up incredible possibilities for expanding your networks. Write down five ways you can use travel (including commuting) to work your people nets. Begin to practice your new travel networking strategies.

3. The dominion mandate includes the creation of cultures and organizations. In what ways do the cultures of the organizations you belong to make networking a part of your job? In what ways do those cultures impede the expansion and proper functioning of networks? Write down one way that you could work to improve the culture of your workplace to enhance the networks crucial to its success.

CHAPTER FIVE

JESUS THE NETWORKER

A s Jesus' successes brought Him into the public eye and as His "busyness/business" increased, He prepared to put together His team. As He did so, He began the serious part of His networking, creating a tight central net strong enough to hold the whole net together.

The New Testament talks about the twelve apostles as a foundation for the church, [61] a good metaphor for conceiving the church as a building. If you conceive the church as a net, you can imagine the design of another network structure—a spider web— in which the connections are much closer at the center and get farther apart as the web widens. The center has to remain tight to maintain the web; and as Jesus set out to call His first disciples, He chose people with whom He wanted to spend a great deal of time. Mark 3:14 declares the purpose Jesus had in calling the disciples: "He appointed twelve *that they might be with him* and that he might send them out to preach" (emphasis added).

FISHING FOR PEOPLE

We've already seen that Jesus issued His first call to fishermen. When a large crowd that came to hear Him preach virtually pushed Him into the water, He asked Peter, James, and John to take Him into their boat so He could speak just off shore. And soon He created in their world what He had just experienced in His own—an overwhelming catch of fish. Peter didn't, perhaps, understand the significance of the huge crowd, but he fully understood the meaning of the net-breaking catch of fish. "Go away from me, Lord; I am a sinful man!" he said. [62] Jesus responded, "Don't be afraid; from now on you will fish for people." [63]

Don't be afraid? Was Jesus kidding? How could Peter *not* tremble with fear? First, he realized that the holy man to whom he had committed himself had the power of God at His disposal. In contrast, as a vile and sinful person, Peter knew he didn't deserve the privilege of walking with Jesus.

NETWORKING TIP

No one who has not realized the fact of his or her own sinful unworthiness is ready to take on the work of the kingdom net.

Unworthiness feels daunting enough, but the situation suggested more than that. Jesus essentially said to Peter, "The same thing you just saw in the boat, you will now see on the land—among people! You are going to enter a life that will rip your networks to shreds."

If you thought of this book as another *How to Win Friends and Influence People*—a self-help book that will teach you to win everyone over—I'm sorry. Following Jesus does *not* mean learning how to make friends with everyone.

Just as Jesus had enemies who constantly sought to unravel His work, so you may also pay a relational price for your commitment to the kingdom net.

The "cultured despisers of religion," as the liberal theologian Schleiermacher called them, as well as the less sophisticated party-animal kind of God-resisters, may include members of your own family. Both of these groups may bitterly oppose you. In Luke 18:28, Peter commented on the effect the kingdom had had on him and the other disciples: "We have left all we had to follow you!" Jesus recognized his statement as true, and responded, "Truly I tell you, no one who has left home or wife or brothers or sisters or parents or children for the sake of the kingdom of God will fail to receive many times as much in this age, and in the age to come eternal life." [64]

As Jesus had promised, the kingdom ripped Peter's relational networks apart, just as the sea had ripped his fishing nets. But at last count, more than 2 billion people across the planet have been added to the kingdom net just in our time.

Even though the kingdom may cost you some relationships, you should not conclude that your submission to God's rule will always alienate you from those who have no faith in Christ. Some Christians have adopted such a knee-jerk, separatist attitude that they wind up becoming the alienators rather than merely the alienated. Whatever you do, don't live your Christian life in a way that unnecessarily alienates those who haven't yet entered the kingdom.

NETWORKING TIP

The price we pay in broken relationships will hurt us emotionally, but the relationships we establish in the kingdom net will be a worthy reward for our sacrifice.

Regardless of your occupation—whether you're a doctor, a bus driver, a lawyer, a factory worker, an engineer, a farmer, a businessperson, an artist, or a pastor—your profession is both secular and sacred. All of our callings are sacred, because God is the one who has called us. And they are all secular (i.e. "worldly") because the people God has called us to reach live in the world.

NETWORKING TIP

If you allow your profession of faith to make you uncomfortable and awkward around those who don't share your faith in Christ, you won't succeed in allowing God to use you for expanding the kingdom net.

A minister who sees pastoral work as only sacred, and not also secular, will stunt his or her church and personal life terribly. Too many pastors spend all their time with Christians, dooming them to a form of leadership that remains merely transactional and hardly ever becomes truly transformational.

According to the leadership theory of James McGregor Burns, most leadership is merely transactional. In other words, leaders trade their performance for goods and services their followers can offer them. So maybe a pastor offers preaching, coordination of religious rituals like the sacraments, weddings, funerals, and other services, in exchange for a place of honor in the community, a (usually) small salary, and perhaps a manse to live in. Transactional pastors place a strong emphasis on maintaining the church's traditions and the status quo. They seldom call on the people in their church to do anything hard or sacrificial, and the people don't really expect their pastor to do much, either. The church doesn't grow, people don't routinely come to Christ through the church's ministry, and no one experiences transformation. Over time, the church population grows older and older . . . and in time . . . it disappears.

By contrast, transformational leadership centers on a transforming vision. The leader calls on the community to make sacrifices and take risks to achieve the vision. If the vision involves evangelism, the church calls on its members to spend time not only with Christians, but also with people who have not yet entered the kingdom.

When pastors spend all their time with Christians, you can safely bet that the members of their congregations will do the same. Some churches even make strong efforts to get Christians to do business primarily with other Christians and to avoid doing business with people outside their Christian circle. It sounds like a great formula for creating lawsuits between Christians, but not a sound business or evangelistic strategy!

A pastor friend of mine, an extremely effective evangelist, requires all of his staff to cultivate friendships with unbelievers. He knows they'll never bring people to Christ unless they talk to people who don't know Christ. As part of their job reports, they must describe how and with whom they are building friendships outside the church. As a result, over the past ten years, the church has multiplied five times in membership.

Some might claim they have a calling to minister inside the church rather than evangelize those who don't yet know the Lord. I have no doubt that some people have a calling to work primarily with believers, for example, to teach in a Christian college or school, or to manage a Christian compassion agency, or to lead a Christian denomination. These kinds of agencies play important roles in the kingdom and have great value for a variety of reasons. And people in these kinds of vocations will often spend more time with Christians than with non-Christians. But even they must realize that their "Christian work" can *never* take the place of the mission of God. It can support and aid others who focus on evangelism, but it can never relieve them of the basic kingdom calling to share their faith in Christ with those who haven't yet experienced the reality and power of His rule. Those who work full-time in Christian businesses and agencies must take extra care to maintain opportunities to meet, befriend, and influence people who need a saving encounter with the Lord.

LOVING LEPERS (AND OTHERS) CONTAGIOUSLY

After calling His disciples—people who clearly had skills useful in building the kingdom net—Jesus encountered a person no one considered useful to the kingdom. In that encounter, He healed a leper. [65]

Lepers were the ultimate social pariahs of Jesus' time, and no one recommended befriending lepers as a valid networking strategy. Jesus, however, employed this strategy to great effect. Not only lepers, but every other kind of "useless person" you can imagine became valuable threads in the kingdom net. Jesus even specifically called on His disciples to befriend such people. In the parable of the great banquet, Jesus said:

> "When you give a luncheon or dinner, do not invite your friends, your brothers or sisters, your relatives, or your rich neighbors; if you do, they may invite you back and so you will be repaid. But when you give a banquet, invite the poor, the crippled, the lame, the blind, and you will be blessed. Although they cannot repay you, you will be repaid at the resurrection of the righteous." [66]

As a university president, I frequently host dinners in my home for distinguished guests. When my amazing wife, Kathleen, doesn't cook, we employ chefs like Jason Jones to come to our home. One way or the other, we serve up some of the finest meals available on Seattle's tony East Side. I love getting to know highly successful Christians because they tend to be extremely interesting people who have achieved things in areas I want to grow in myself.

I also need their counsel and friendship to help our university fulfill the vision God has given us.

On the other hand, we often invite students and other people who are not wealthy to our place for home-cooked meals. Wealth owns no monopoly on wisdom! I always say that every time I listen to students, I get smarter. They teach me just as much as older and wealthier people do, and I need their advice to succeed in my work.

Periodically I go out late at night with some wealthy friends. They love the Lord and they love people. We volunteer with one of Seattle's rescue missions to seek out homeless people. We give them food, invite them back to the shelter, and offer other kinds of assistance. But they seem to appreciate most our talking to them and listening to their stories. We ask them questions, hear their wisdom, and even take their advice. Honoring them in their poverty dignifies our relative wealth just as much as, or perhaps more than, our gifts dignify their poverty.

Kingdom people don't measure net worth by financial statements. Kingdom people cultivate friendships from every level of wealth, social class, educational attainment level, occupation, IQ (intellectual quotient), EQ (emotional intelligence), and HQ (no not headquarters, but rather *humor quotient*—not all people are equally funny!). I spent most of my adult life living in the Third World, developing deep friendships from the top of society to the bottom. All those friends have contributed something important to my life and work for God.

The point of Jesus' parable has little to do with banquets and food. It focuses on the friendships involved. What good does it do to throw a banquet for the poor if inwardly you despise them? Most poor people would have the dignity to stop coming to your banquets if they knew they were getting mocked in the kitchen or in your planning sessions. Jesus is making a point about the openness of our hearts to the poor and the despised and the sick and disabled.

An open heart is contagious. God starts it out, loving every single one of us first. God's love in us spills over into love for others. As we love others, other people catch the Spirit and start loving them as well. Love turns quickly to service, and service leads to joy. Serving food turns a meeting into a party. Hospitality turns fear and doubt into comfort and joy. Just as hatred can start a conflict that escalates into war, so love can escalate even more. Loving lepers, and other people no one else loves, can spread like a divine contagion.

Jesus went to great lengths to make this point of equal love and hospitality, but my favorite episode along these lines appears in Luke 16:1–31. The chapter starts with the parable of the shrewd manager, a wasteful administrator who gets fired from his job by a rich proprietor. [67] Knowing that he has little time, he decides to use his remaining power in a final accounting to make friends for himself. By shrewd systemic discounting, he settles up the outstanding accounts, in the process gaining favor with his boss's creditors. He hopes he will be able to convert that favor to cash and some new opportunities.

Surprisingly, Jesus *commended* the shrewdness of the manager, then added:

> For the people of this world are more shrewd in dealing
> with their own kind than are the people of the light. I tell
> you, use worldly wealth to gain friends for yourselves,

so that when it is gone, you will be welcomed into eternal dwellings. [68]

Note the clear networking implications here. Just as the people of this world shrewdly network (dealing with their own kind), so we should shrewdly network for the kingdom (dealing with our own kind). Jesus said it explicitly: gain friends for yourself who will welcome you into eternal dwellings; or as we might say: the final consummation and full manifestation of the kingdom. Now *that's* networking for the kingdom!

OUR KIND OF PEOPLE

So we must ask, "Who are our 'own kind'?" The phrase sounds ugly when used in high society. Most of us cringe at those who say, "So and so just isn't our kind of people." But there is such a thing as "our kind of people" for those who have joined the kingdom net. Who are they?

The rest of Luke 16 tells us that poor, sick Lazarus is "our kind of people," and not the privileged man who neglected him. In Luke's version of the Beatitudes, Jesus included the poor, the hungry, those who weep, the hated, the excluded, and the reviled among those blessed in the kingdom. [69] He specifically excluded the rich, the full, the laughers, and the greatly admired. Why? Does God hate the rich, the powerful, and the successful?

Not at all. In fact, God specifically includes some rich folk among "our kind of people." In Luke 18:9–14, Jesus told the parable of the Pharisee and the tax collector. Both were rich, but only one was the kingdom kind. The reader would naturally expect

Jesus to name the rich Pharisee, and not the rich tax collector, as "our kind." But, no—while the religious leader revealed a proud and self-righteous heart, the tax collector displayed a broken and repentant one. Neither money, position, nor a state of legal holiness makes someone the kingdom kind, but rather the way one responds to the message of God's rule.

Note the story of Zacchaeus in Luke 19:1–10, a tale that drives home the point of the parable through the life of a real person. (I have written about Zacchaeus at length in other places, e.g., *Your Deepest Dream,* NavPress, 2011.) Despite his ill-gotten riches, Zacchaeus saw the presence of Jesus and the preaching of the kingdom as good news, prompting him to repent and give himself fully to God's rule. Anyone who hears the message of the kingdom as good news and responds to it in humble repentance is "the kingdom kind."

NETWORKING TIP

In our networking for the kingdom, we should offer a hand of friendship to people of all kinds.

Favoritism has no place in the kingdom. Poor and rich people, strong and disabled, healthy and sick, esteemed and despised, all these types and more can hear the kingdom as good news or as bad. Jesus placed special attention on the inclusion of the weak and despised. He knew that people acting according to their sinful human nature could easily overlook them and their needs. He also knew that they would most likely hear the proclamation of the kingdom as good news. When the world mistreats you, the news of its overthrow sounds like good news indeed.

You may have started on the road to great success in your career. Perhaps God has blessed you with education, opportunity, talent, and a context in which you plan to carry out the call of God on your life. You should go to great lengths, because Jesus did, to avoid overlooking the weak as you work your section of the kingdom net.

Aesop's Fables, a pre-Christian source of wisdom from ancient Greece, tells the story of the Lion and the Mouse. I've known it all my life, as perhaps you have. The fable describes how a weak and tiny mouse freed a strong and arrogant lion from a hunter's snare because the lion had previously had mercy on him. The Bible makes the same point in Ecclesiastes:

> The race is not to the swift
> nor the battle to the strong,
> nor does food come to the wise
> nor wealth to the brilliant
> nor favor to the learned;
> but time and chance happen to them all.
> Moreover, no one knows when their hour will come:
> As fish are caught in a cruel net,
> or birds are taken in a snare,
> so people are trapped by evil times
> that fall unexpectedly upon them. [70]

Mere prudence tells us that sometimes we need the friendship of the weak to be rescued in our hour of trouble. But that's not the point. The kingdom net works both ways. In our networking for the kingdom, people need us and we need them.

The kingdom of God has no room for those who think of anyone as beneath them. God is above us all, and the rest of the kingdom net is lateral.

Jesus' healing of the leper resulted in a flurry of publicity among the social networks of Jerusalem. While Jesus told the leper to tell no one except the priest about his healing, He explicitly instructed the leper to do it "as a testimony to them." In so doing, the leper became a high level operative in the kingdom net, taking the message of the kingdom directly to the highest religious authorities in Jerusalem. And since the miracle had taken place in public, it set off an immediate wave of publicity that spread throughout Jerusalem. The "useless" leper wound up being a highly useful witness of the coming of the kingdom in Jesus.

WITHDRAWAL TO PRAY

The power of momentum contributes greatly to professional success. Once you have "Big Mo" working for you, you want to keep it going. The Proverbs say that a disgraceful son sleeps during harvest time, and no person who values achievement wants anything to do with laziness. [71] We all want to "make hay while the sun is shining." But commitment to the priority of feeding "Big Mo" is not an absolute value. We also must know when to step back and rest.

Although Jesus was at the very beginning of His ministry and nowhere close to "burning out," Luke says He withdrew to lonely places and prayed. [72] In fact, the Bible says He made this His regular practice. If you want to maintain personal health, passion and energy for your professional work and calling, and also maintain a happy marriage and family, then you have to prioritize rest and prayer and solitude.

NETWORKING TIP

Sometimes you have to shut down the network for maintenance.

Computer network professionals know the value of periodically shutting down their systems. They tend to shut down their networks—to do the upgrades and repairs needed to keep functioning effectively—whenever demand dips to its lowest point. The same is true for kingdom networking. We must take time for solitude, prayer, and rest. What good does a vast network of friends and acquaintances do you if your constant, frenetic networking drives you to a nervous breakdown, a moral failure, or a heart attack?

The human soul cannot keep pouring out energy and affection and action into the lives of others without taking time for recharging. While some people feel recharged by being with friends and coworkers and others find that social networking depletes them, even the most gregarious extrovert cannot keep recharging on the fly forever. Some things in the human soul, such as holiness and intellectual depth, get recharged only by spending time in quiet solitude, meditation, and prayer.

If we don't take time for depth recharging, we doom ourselves to superficiality. If the image on the surface doesn't reflect deep health and spirituality, then we cannot sustain our activities. Jesus knew it, and during His sojourn in a flesh-and-bone human body, He made it a habit to shut down the network regularly to pray. (You may rest assured that He's no longer subject to human breakdown, and the kingdom net itself never shuts down!)

A DETERMINED TEAM OF FRIENDS

As Luke's narrative of the early ministry of Jesus continues, a remarkable event occurred that says powerful things about our own networking. As Jesus taught inside a house, He exercised great power over sickness, and word got out about His healing power. As a result:

> Some men came carrying a paralyzed man on a mat and tried to take him into the house to lay him before Jesus. When they could not find a way to do this because of the crowd, they went up on the roof and lowered him on his mat through the tiles into the middle of the crowd, right in front of Jesus. When Jesus saw their faith, he said, "Friend, your sins are forgiven." [73]

I have always found fascinating the depth of friendship and determination these men demonstrated in getting their friend into the presence of Jesus. Why would they go to such lengths? The text doesn't tell us, so it probably doesn't matter. Had they been friends for a long time? Were family members involved? Had the man suffered from paralysis his whole life, or had he suffered an accident?

My overactive imagination whispers that the man had become a paralytic due to some riotous living, since Jesus focuses on forgiving his sins rather than on healing his body. Could one of the friends who lifted him up and then lowered him down to Jesus been present at, and perhaps even responsible for, the accident that left him paralyzed? Did a sense of guilt motivate the friend to help? Luke addressed none of those things. He did, however, clearly indicate that *faith* motivated the helpers. Their faith moved Jesus to exercise His saving and healing power, canceling the curse of sin and restoring life and health to the lame man.

Luke certainly had no intention of saying anything about networking here. But someone did some networking to make this story possible. Someone, whether the paralytic or one of his friends, called together the group of faith-filled friends who would stop at nothing until they got the man to Jesus. These men turned out, along with Jesus, to be the best friends the paralytic ever had. Their example reveals the essence of kingdom networking.

NETWORKING TIP

Our ultimate goal in building our networks is to put together working relationships that will bring people to Jesus.

Most people seem to assume that we can live compartmentalized lives in which we leave Jesus at home or at church. Many Christians don't welcome Jesus into their workplace. As a result, we share Jesus with our friends who already believe in Him, and we don't share Jesus with those who don't believe in Him. But kingdom networking won't flow on that short circuit!

On the other hand, kingdom networking doesn't imply that we must turn our workplace into a site of direct evangelism. While some workplaces would see such activity as perfectly appropriate, others would consider it an unwelcome distraction to both coworkers and employers. In some situations, a professional would act in an unethical way by directly leading a coworker to Christ in a purely linear, one-on-one encounter. An overzealous boss should never pressure an employee to come to Christ! The ends of evangelism do not justify all means.

So what's the alternative? If we cannot share Christ directly with someone in our workplace, we can create opportunities to engage coworkers, customers, or clients off the job in ways that make it possible for them to know Christ. We might invite them, off the clock, to services at our church or to some Christian event. Such a relatively direct, linear way, however, will not always yield the best result. In most cases, successful evangelism and disciple-making call for a more complete relationship than exists in most workplace environments.

Developing full-fledged friendships, complete with shared activities outside of religious activities, almost always bears the ripest fruit. Such activities might include helping people move into their houses, playing golf, attending sporting events, making quilts, playing in the local civic symphony, or getting active in a civic organization such as Rotary International. The options are as diverse as human interests.

As real relationships develop, the reality of Christ in our lives begins to emerge. Sometimes, deeper relationships allow us to share our kingdom networks with people in ways that benefit them professionally or personally in completely nonspiritual aspects. As we support them with our prayers and engage them with the kingdom net, we will eventually touch them spiritually as well. No matter what else we do to bring our coworkers to Christ, we should be faithful to pray for them.

How much trouble will we risk to bring people to Christ? The men who carried the paralytic to Jesus overcame crowds, heights, and brick walls. It took real effort. But they felt determined to bring that man to Jesus, no matter what. "Jesus saw their faith," the text says, and He saved and healed the paralyzed man. As a result, "Everyone was amazed and gave praise to God. They were filled with awe and said, 'We have seen remarkable things today.'" [74] When we carry our neighbors' needs and burdens, we, too, will see remarkable things.

THE REST OF THE STORY

In the remainder of Luke, Jesus kept expanding the kingdom net, calling tax collectors like Levi and Zacchaeus to repentance and forgiveness and a changed life that put their skills to work in new ways. He interacted with sinful people and religious people, powerful people and the oppressed, the sick and the healthy. He received crucial support from a young boy with a few loaves and fishes, which He multiplied to feed a large crowd. He had a meal with just about everyone! In all these encounters, He conducted a master class in human relations. Given the spectacular spread of Christianity since Jesus first began to declare the kingdom net, the wise networker will make the study of Jesus' way of dealing with people his best textbook on networking.

WORKING THE NET

1. Contrary to many myths, homeless people are much like you and me. They aren't more likely to suffer from mental illness than people with homes. They are more likely to abuse drugs, but that often results from homelessness, rather than causing it. If you live in a city, find out what agencies work in your area to help homeless people. Call and ask if they could use volunteer help. Get a friend to go with you and spend a few hours volunteering. You may get to serve food to hungry people. If so, ask questions about their life stories, their friends, their hopes. Learn their names. If you can network with homeless people, you are halfway to expanding your networking range.

2. Choose a civic organization in your community and attend one of its meetings. You can find out on the Internet when it meets or ask among your friends to find out who belongs to one. It might be the Rotary Club or a similar service organization, such as the Chamber of Commerce, the local Republican or Democrat club, a Parent-Teacher Association at your children's school, or some other organization. If you don't normally attend church, you might choose a church organization. When you attend the meeting, introduce yourself to the officers of the club. If there is a guest speaker, take advantage of the opportunity to meet her or him. Doing this will help you meet leaders in your community—both Christians and non-Christians. If you enjoy the meeting, keep attending and meet more members of the organization. Consider joining, after attending two or three times. Serve as a volunteer, and soon you will have some new network connections.

CHAPTER SIX

DO

NETWORK MAINTENANCE

I
t does little good to build a network if you don't maintain it. The fact that you've met someone doesn't mean that you've established a useful connection. Sometimes you can establish a working connection through a single meeting; sometimes that single meeting will yield negligible results. In most cases, it will take intentional follow-up to create a working connection.

Once you've established a relationship of admiration and trust, you've gained a valuable asset for the kingdom net. And now you'll want to safeguard those opportunities by maintaining them.

THREE MODES OF MAINTENANCE

You'll use three main modes to maintain your network: *remote touches, face-to-face meetings,* and *gift giving.* Remote touches employ resources like notes on Internet-based social media, text messages, written notes, and telephone calls. Face-to-face meetings, by definition, require physical presence but vary in time commitments. Gift giving can occur in either remote or face-to-face modes. It may include anything from buying coffee or a meal to giving a wrist watch or some luxury item.

REMOTE TOUCHES

Jim Wellborn is a master of the remote touch. I met Jim at a youth camp when he was a college student and I was twelve years old. He came to my church to spend the weekend with others his age. A few years later, he became the District Youth Director for my denomination in Alaska, and I reconnected with him on a missionary trip to Honduras. As his career advanced, he joined the staff of the national resource office of our church, directing a program that coordinated short-term missions for youth. Unbelievably, he remembered me. As my career matured, he brought a missionary team to visit the church I pastored as a missionary in El Salvador.

At that point, Jim and I had established a collegial relationship. Since that time, he has sent me countless text messages. Every time he thinks about me, he sends a note. If he finds that we plan to visit the same place, he'll see if we can connect. Sometimes he wants to let me know about something he believes I'd have an interest in. He knows I like him, and he likes me. We are not "bosom buddies." We have probably never had a deeply personal conversation. But I know that I matter to him, and he to me. If

> **NO ONE EVER SAYS, "I WISH I HADN'T RECEIVED THAT WORD OF ENCOURAGEMENT!"**

he needs a favor, he knows I'll do everything I can to help him. He has won my good regard by consistently reaching out to me for forty years. You can do the same by genuinely expressing interest in people over time.

When should you make remote touches? Examples include when a friend or acquaintance:

1. has sent you a gift or spent time with you
2. celebrates a birthday or anniversary
3. receives a newborn child or grandchild into their family
4. publishes a book or article that you notice
5. is announced as a speaker at a conference
6. receives some public honor
7. gets mentioned in the media
8. comes to your mind randomly
9. comes up on your intentional networking plan

To know when someone is celebrating a birthday or anniversary, check out social media like Facebook. Many people publish that information on their profiles. Facebook will alert you to these events. If you merge your contacts with Facebook, your smart phone will remind you of their significant days. In the course of your daily work and reading, people's names will emerge that you know. Make it a habit to congratulate people on their achievements, whether professional, civic, religious, familial, or of some other type.

Everyone likes to receive congratulations on victories and successes and rites of passage. No one ever says, "I wish I hadn't received that word of encouragement!" No matter how humble or relatively unknown you may be, remember that everyone likes to receive positive words.

FACE-TO-FACE MEETINGS

With the advent of Internet-based social media, we can send almost unlimited messages to keep in touch with people. But we have limited time on this side of heaven, so we can't meet often enough with the friends and the people we admire. That scarcity of time makes face-to-face meetings especially valuable.

Face-to-face meetings come in an almost limitless variety of forms. A base-level form is an office appointment. When visiting a person in their office, especially if for the first time, demonstrate that you value the time the individual gives you. Determine ahead of time the amount of time you want to stay, even when you make the appointment. A purely social meeting might call for no more than fifteen minutes. If your host wants you to stay longer, he or she will insist that you do so as soon as you say, "Thanks for making time to meet with me. I know you're busy. I'd better let you get back to work."

If you've come to make a formal proposal or to discuss a complicated issue, you may need as much as an hour or more. Just set the time limits in advance and don't exceed that time unless your host insists. Regardless how long you planned to stay, the meeting has ended when your host closes his or her notebook and stands up. He or she will say, "Thanks for coming," or "I'm sorry, but I have to move on to the next appointment," or make some other comment that closes the discussion.

Such closing behavior doesn't mean your host doesn't want to talk to you. It often means exactly what he or she said. He has other tasks to attend. She has other people to see. At that point, you stand, say "thank-you," and extend your hand warmly. Say no more than a couple of sentences as you move out of the office. Those couple of sentences should not continue your discussion, which ended when your host stood up. Just say a couple of personal things like, "Please say hi to (so and so) for me." You might also suggest meeting again at some time in the future.

Meeting for coffee or a meal provides another useful form of personal visit. Courtesy says that whoever makes the invitation should also pick up the tab. Breaking bread together is a powerful form of making friends. Even a brief examination of Jesus' networking style reveals that He spent a lot of time eating with people. From the wedding at Cana to the post-resurrection breakfast on the beach, Jesus regularly shared food and drink with people, in small groups and huge crowds. Luke recorded at least ten occasions when Jesus ate with someone. When He fed the 4,000 men [75] and the 5,000 men [76] (plus women and children!), He even declared Himself to be "the Bread of Life." [77] It makes sense that the ultimate memorial of Jesus is Holy Communion, a ceremonial sharing of food and drink. [78] You can tie the kingdom net around you with powerful knots if you make a habit of regularly meeting with people for food or drink.

> **EVEN A BRIEF EXAMINATION OF JESUS' NETWORKING STYLE REVEALS THAT HE SPENT A LOT OF TIME EATING WITH PEOPLE.**

Another effective way of building relationships is to enjoy events together. If you know a person loves cultural events, suggest that you attend a symphony orchestra concert together with your spouses. If your friend plays golf or another sport you enjoy, get together for a game. Some people like camping, fishing, hunting, hiking, biking, paintball, tennis, shopping, crafts, and other activities. Try to schedule things you actually like to do, rather than doing something just so you can hang out with a contact.

This principle rings especially true when playing sports with people. I've learned to share things I like rather than trying to do things I'm absolutely no good at. People usually don't make a good impression on others in completely unfamiliar situations or when doing activities they either don't like or don't understand.

In the kingdom net, taking people to church with you or visiting their church with them can generate extremely powerful results. When you get God involved in your relationships, you have a much better chance of avoiding shallow connections. Nothing engages and activates the kingdom net more than the manifest presence of God. Some of the most powerful spiritual experiences I've ever had resulted from friends taking me to church.

You can experience no greater joy than introducing people to Christ. Don't be shy in sharing your faith! Still, make sure you never place unwarranted pressure on business associates in trying to get them to go to church with you. Freely invite people to join you for worship, but let them freely accept or decline your invitation. You'll gain the right sense of when to invite people to church only when you make enough attempts at it. You might also consider inviting people to join you at a Bible study, a faith-at-work group, a marriage seminar or other topical event, or any other kind of faith-oriented meeting. If they have a life-changing experience at church with you, they'll never forget your role in facilitating the event.

Your home can provide the most powerful venue for kingdom networking. In the same way, people feel open to you when you visit their home. As I've mentioned, Kathleen and I have always kept a steady stream of people coming through our home.

> **FREELY INVITE PEOPLE TO JOIN YOU FOR WORSHIP, BUT LET THEM FREELY ACCEPT OR DECLINE YOUR INVITATION.**

Friends from all over the world have visited with us there. If you choose to use this networking tool, however, you shouldn't expect people to reciprocate. In the great majority of cases, your guests won't extend an invitation to their own homes. Such a situation doesn't mean that your guests didn't enjoy coming to your home or that they wouldn't accept another invitation. It just means that not everyone feels equally comfortable in the host role.

Never take it personally if people don't reciprocate your expressions of hospitality and interest. Some people really are shy. Not everyone is a people person, and people have a wide range of capacity for friendship. Not everyone will want a closer connection with you. You won't catch a fish on every cast. Don't get emotional about it. Networking is no place for personal insecurity to rule. Develop a thick hide and stay focused on successful connections, not on failed ones.

When I was a boy, I used to go fishing nearly every day along with my brother, Randy. We would sit on the creek bank for hours and catch nothing. It didn't matter. Fishing was its own reward. As millions have said: A bad day fishing is better than a good day at work. If you become a great kingdom networker, you'll never spend another day "at work" again. Every day will be a fishing day!

Traveling together with someone offers yet another powerful form of personal meeting. When people travel together, they feel more open than at any other time. People become especially vulnerable when they travel. So if you intend to network by traveling with someone, take care to be on your best behavior. You can hurt people's feelings or display your own hurt feelings in ways that devastate an ongoing relationship. Gender issues also come into play, so prepare for tricky situations if you travel with someone of the opposite gender. Beware the many pitfalls! But don't discount the rich benefits of traveling with colleagues and friends.

Let me offer a few items of advice for those who plan to travel with colleagues. Not everyone will agree with my perspective, and everyone has to use their own best discretion. Make your own rules, but don't make them alone. Discuss them with your colleagues so everyone will be on the same page (or at least know what page everyone else is on).

1. Travel goes best when done in groups bigger than two. Having a third person along provides many benefits, including a witness that nothing inappropriate has occurred, another person to relieve the conversational burden, and more people to benefit from the trip. As the old saying goes: The more the merrier.

2. When people of opposite gender travel together, include a third person to ensure propriety. I've

seen people ruin their marriages with colleagues on business trips. Even if you trust yourself completely, don't trust what others will say about you. In business, you may find that you absolutely must travel "alone" with a colleague of the opposite gender. If so, maintain your professional demeanor in an exceedingly scrupulous way. In the ministry, don't even *consider* traveling alone with a colleague of the opposite gender, but do make sure that your personal travel rules don't shut out the other gender from the councils of power.

3. Pay the extra money to have your own hotel room on business trips. This measure protects you from bad appearances. If you plan to travel in a large group in which everyone will share rooms, the context offers sufficient protection of your reputation, so go ahead and share a room with a person of the same gender.

4. Build some time in business trips for a bit of tourism or play. If you will travel "on the company's nickel," know the rules for spending business funds on entertainment. Entertainment that includes clients is often chargeable to the company or tax-deductible as a business expense for self-employed people. Entertainment that doesn't include clients becomes a trickier issue. Play by the rules, and even if it costs you some personal funds, take the opportunity to have a good time when traveling. Beautiful or fascinating places and fun activities

provide shared experiences from which great relationships can emerge.

GIFT GIVING

What a wonderful privilege to give gifts to build a relationship! Everyone loves to receive gifts, and sales representatives consider it standard practice to give gifts to business associates and potential clients. Always give networking gifts out of real admiration, sincerity, and the joy of giving. Kingdom networking must avoid manipulation of all kinds, and gift giving can serve as a form of manipulation. Guard your heart in such matters!

I like to make creative gifts, which can demonstrate a higher level of sincerity than ready-made gifts. For example, I have a long habit of giving a silver coin, preferably a silver dollar or half dollar, to friends or people I admire who become new college presidents. I always choose a coin from the year in which their college was founded, purchase a coin case for it, and have it engraved with their name, the date of their inauguration, and the name of their institution. I then write a note to accompany the gift. I usually include a prayer that their investment of time will grow in value over time, just as the silver coin has increased in value since the year of their college's founding. When you give such a gift, people will never throw it away, and it will remind them of your thoughtfulness for years.

> **KINGDOM NETWORKING MUST AVOID MANIPULATION OF ALL KINDS.**

I once invited a public official to participate in an important academic event that required the use of academic regalia. Because I knew that ethics rules wouldn't permit the official to accept a monetary honorarium, I asked him whether we could give him the academic regalia he needed to wear. Most people who don't plan to become faculty members don't buy such expensive regalia. The official didn't own regalia, even though he often spoke at such events. We ordered official regalia from the prestigious school where he had graduated. Now, whenever he attends academic events, he can proudly use the hooded robe and tam we gave him, and he'll think about us. He'll also remember our sincere thankfulness and high regard for him. Everyone wins.

Thoughtful, creative gifts can take any form imaginable. Take time to think about the significance of a person's life and work and choose a gift that expresses your feelings. Thoughtful gifts beat gift certificates every time. You know the principle: it's not the gift, but the thought that counts. When the gift clearly expresses the thought, the memory of your thoughts will last as long as the gift does.

NETWORK MAINTENANCE PLANNING

No matter how much of a people person you are, or how natural networking comes to you, you'll want to supplement casual efforts at networking with an *intentional networking plan*. Every person has equal and absolute value before God, and every person deserves our hallowed respect as one made in God's image. Nevertheless, we all move in relative circles of intimacy. Everyone has people they should see every day, every week, every month, every year, every couple of years, every ten years, etc.

> **"AN INTENTIONAL NETWORKING PLAN HELPS YOU ESTABLISH HOW OFTEN TO CONTACT THE VARIOUS PEOPLE IN YOUR NETWORK, AND WHAT LEVEL OF CONTACT YOU SHOULD MAKE."**

An intentional networking plan helps you establish how often to contact the various people in your network, and what level of contact you should make. As relationships change, your plan will change, with people moving both inward and outward in the concentric circles of intimacy.

The inner ring of intimacy involves the close circle of people you see every day or every week. You usually don't need to include them in a formal plan. (If you're a married man, you may want to plan things like sending flowers or other gifts to your wife. If you're a married woman, you may want to remind yourself to send random love notes to your husband.)

If you don't already use a computerized calendar or other software to organize your activities, you may want to start using Microsoft Outlook or an equivalent program. You can use electronic calendars to set how often you want an appointment to recur. If you still rely on a paper calendar, you'll have to reinvent your plan every year. So go ahead and move on to an electronic calendar; then you'll stop wasting so much time doing everything manually. Few people have time to waste, and it won't take long to learn this new tool.

As you make your plan, you'll need to decide (1) the *type of contact* you think you should make, and (2) the *frequency* with which you want to engage your contacts. Again, types of contacts include remote touches and face-to-face meetings, which may occur monthly, quarterly, semi-annually, or annually.

Start with your closest circle, which probably includes people you work with or people you consider close friends. For the most part, you don't need to include your inner circle in your intentional plan. But sometimes, you'll want to schedule touches purposefully among your closest contacts. For example, three or four times a week I chat with a friend on the opposite coast of the United States. Either I call him, or he calls me. He is perhaps my closest friend outside my family. We don't need to schedule our phone calls. On the other hand, we usually get together twice a year when one of us travels to the other's city. Such visits require some advance thought and should have a place on your network maintenance plan. If you struggle to remember birthdays and anniversaries and the like, or if you find yourself always shopping for Christmas gifts at the last moment, you can include reminders to plan your gifts. Most items related to your inner circle don't belong in the intentional plan, but a few items may.

Other contacts deserve a monthly touch. To ensure that you make those touches, put reminder notes in your calendar once a month. The same goes for contacts that you want to make less frequently. Plot them out on your electronic calendar. In some cases, you can set appointments for face-to-face or phone calls directly. In others, you can make yourself a note to call or send a note or make face-to-face appointments at different times in the year. If you have an administrative assistant, ask that person to make such appointments for you.

Sales people use a wide selection of "contact management software" that networkers may find useful as well. The emergence of smart phones and their helpful apps has greatly helped professionals organize and execute their network maintenance plans. Searching mobile app stores with the term "networking" offers a variety of options. Some apps perform better than others. Nothing can really replace your calendar, but the ideal app would translate your network maintenance plan directly into your calendar (app developers take note!).

WORKING THE NET

This is the granddaddy of all end-of-chapter exercises, and the one that has the biggest potential for the formal organization of your network maintenance.

1. Figure out what categories of networking relationships best fit your various activities. For example, you may choose categories such as "Personal Friend," "Church," "Rotary," "Colleagues," "Professional," "Clients," and many more.

2. Define categories for desired frequency of contact. You might choose "Weekly," "Monthly," "Quarterly," "Semi-Annually," and "Annually."

3. Assuming that you use Microsoft Outlook for contact management, go to "contacts" and click on "categorize" on the menu bar. (If you use another program or app, the process will look similar.) You can create new categories by clicking on "new."

4. After you have added all your newly defined categories from (1) and (2) above, you have two options. You can go through all your contacts and categorize each one by clicking on the same menu icon that you used in (3). If you have a large list of contacts, such a task may feel too daunting to consider. Even if you have an assistant, a large list of contacts will take time (and money) to process. A second option is to think through the frequency categories and make a list of the people you want to include in each category. Perhaps Dunbar's Number of about

150 is the maximum number of contacts you want to assign to a contact frequency, or perhaps you will start with a much smaller number. Choose a set number of weekly contacts, perhaps five. Do the same with each frequency group.

5. Assuming you chose the second option, you will be able to assign each of your chosen contacts to the categories one at a time, defining the type of contact as well as the frequency with which you want to touch base with them.

6. Once you have organized your contacts, sort them by frequency and then start making calendar appointments for the people with whom you want to connect. Choose the kind of face-to-face or remote contact you want to make, as discussed in the chapter.

7. Start making a contact with people on a planned, regular basis.

CHAPTER SEVEN

THINK

THE GREAT COMMISSION

esse Owens is a Spirit-gifted evangelist. [79] He lives to bring other people to Jesus, and he's extremely effective at it. As a preacher, he has an incredible gift for moving people to a decision to follow Christ.

When I was fourteen years old, I met Jesse at the youth camp I attended every summer. I liked him and his ministry, so for years I kept his business card. As a college student, I saw an article in a national church magazine about the church he had founded in Princeton, New Jersey. It impressed me that the church had grown rapidly from an original group of 29 to about 500 members in just a few years in one of the most famous academic towns in America. I had no idea I would ever live in Princeton, but I remembered the story with a great deal of satisfaction.

A couple of years later, I found myself accepted as a student at Princeton Theological Seminary. In need of a place to do the required "field education," as well as needing a part-time job,

I remembered that article and called Jesse Owens on the phone. I told him about meeting him nearly a decade earlier and about how much I had enjoyed his ministry and how proud I felt for his success in Princeton. Oddly, he thought he remembered me (though it turned out he'd recalled someone else). He essentially hired me over the phone. The fact that I had met Jesse years before and now had become a student at Princeton Seminary motivated me to stick my foot boldly in the door.

Jesse Owens became an important mentor for me. He introduced me to everyone he could over the next few years, helping me to build a network of professionals, politicians, and church officials from whom I still benefit in my kingdom network. While I studied at Princeton Seminary, Jesse hired me as his church's full-time campus minister at Princeton University, where I observed firsthand his amazing evangelistic gifts. I used to joke that he could stand up and read the newspaper and people would rush to give their lives to Christ. But I wasn't really joking.

I'm a preacher, too, and I've had the privilege of seeing many people come to Christ through the invitations I've given. But Jesse doesn't stop evangelizing when he steps down from the pulpit. Everywhere he goes, he leads people to Christ. In restaurants, in city parks, in taxis, buses, boats, airplanes, trains, and any other mode of travel, he goes into the world and makes disciples. He not only leads people to Christ, but he walks with them after they start following the Lord. I've seen many people who follow Jesus, but I've never seen anyone as good as Jesse on "following-up" people for Jesus. Jesse makes sure people tie into the kingdom net by introducing them to those who can support them in their walk with God.

I'm positive that the reason Jesse excels at winning souls is that *he exudes genuine love for everyone he meets.* Having grown up on a small tenant farm in a remote town in North Carolina (think: *Mayberry RFD*), Jesse had no social standing when he left home to strike out on his own in the big city of Washington, DC. Shortly after he arrived, lost and alone, he wound up in a church where he met Jesus. That encounter changed him forever. He quickly proceeded to Zion Bible Institute in East Providence, Rhode Island, to prepare for the ministry of evangelism. [80] At Zion, a faith school, students could attend and trust God to help them pay their school bills. Everyone lived a totally sacrificial life. It stood not far from the prestigious Brown University, but it sat on the other side of the universe in terms of social prestige and wealth.

Starting from nowhere and nothing, Jesse began to network in God's kingdom. He got involved with David and Don Wilkerson on the ground floor of the Teen Challenge ministry in New York City in the 1960s and spent uncounted hours ministering to drug addicts. [81] His natural leadership abilities landed him in pastorates in New Jersey, and his evangelistic skills among young people led to a position as the Youth Director for the Assemblies of God in New Jersey. He became a popular camp speaker all over the country. He built a huge personal network, but never stopped sharing Jesus with every person he met. As part of his evangelistic ministry at one university, he led a student to faith in Christ who would soon become a prominent member of the United States House of Representatives.

After spending almost a year in bed with a sickness that should have ended his life, Jesse came roaring back and felt called to plant a church in Princeton, New Jersey—one of the most sophisticated

> **THE POWER OF GOD'S LOVE WORKING THROUGH GOD'S PEOPLE CAN LITERALLY CREATE THE KINGDOM NET IN FRONT OF OUR EYES.**

academic centers in the world. Though Jesse didn't enjoy the benefits of even a bachelor's degree, he had great success in reaching people for Christ in Princeton. Princeton University professors and students, a Princeton mayor, city officials from nearby cities, and a host of townsfolk from all around came to Christ through his ministry, many of whom have followed him into ministry themselves.

After building a church of 500 members in a town others would have thought impossible to reach, Jesse felt called to throw his net to the world as a missionary evangelist. After a time of ministering in Colombia and Argentina, he moved on to more difficult places. He enjoyed his greatest success as a missionary in planting churches in post-Christian Europe, especially Germany. Jesse could barely speak a word of German, but the love that flows out of his heart and the constant testimony of Jesus compelled hundreds of people in Germany to come to Christ.

Jesse now leads a ministry called Global Renewal, through which he cooperates with Teen Challenge to rescue and rehabilitate drug addicts. Teen Challenge has over a thousand centers in ninety-three countries around the world, and Jesse uses his cell phone to operate a worldwide personal rescue hotline that helps addicts. [82] Recently, when he spoke at Northwest University, he put his phone number on his PowerPoint and handed out dozens of business cards to students. He instructed them to call their addict friends and give them his number. Within hours, he began receiving calls from people he had never met. Over the phone, they got a healing dose of God's love through Jesse, and he pulled strings only he can pull to get them accepted into free treatment centers around the country.

I wish I could say that Jesse has taught me all he knows about networking. We've spent thousands of hours together, but he hasn't taught me all he knows. He has taught me almost everything I know about it. He has taught me the power of walking full of the love of Jesus in the anointing of the Holy Spirit. The power of God's love working through God's people can literally create the kingdom net in front of our eyes. Thousands of people have joined the net by the anointing of the Holy Spirit on Jesse's extraordinary life. But Jesse's way of working the net is not the only way to demonstrate God's love.

THE GREAT COMMISSION

The triple command that forms the human mission—multiply, migrate, and rule—could have fulfilled the mission of God in the world except for one thing: the fall. Before sin entered the human picture, the mission of God charged ahead. The Father sent the Son, the Son sent the Spirit, and the whole Trinity played its role in sending humanity into mission in the world. In Genesis 2, we see Adam and Eve walking with God, naming the animals, taking dominion over their circumstances. We can easily imagine how humanity would have spread throughout the world. Love would bring about reproduction. Reproduction would require migration. Both would require taming lands and plants and animals and building human cultures—a perfectly ideal picture.

The fall, however, threw the mission of God and humanity out of sync. After the curse of Genesis 3, sin compromised each area of the human mission. The pains of childbirth accompanied reproduction. Thorns and thistles and painful toil complicated dominion over the earth. Migration took place in the context of banishment from the garden of God's presence. Human work, out of sync with God, no longer necessarily reflects God's Kingship through God's human regents. In contrast, the "prince of this world" rises up against the rule of God. [83]

THE MISSION OF REDEMPTION

The book of Genesis sadly traces the expansion of the kingdom of darkness along with the growth of the human race. But as it dramatically sketches out our descent into moral chaos, it also lays out the track for God's redeeming mission. To Eve, God promised a seed whose heel would crush the serpent's head. [84] In saving Noah from destruction, God made a covenant with the righteous not to destroy the earth again. [85] In choosing righteous Abraham as the father of the faithful, God promised to build up a great nation; through Abraham's family, every family on earth would be blessed. [86] The rest of the Old Testament follows the story of Abraham and his descendants. The story describes their struggle to recognize God as King and express the rule of God in the world, despite the interference of worldly schemes and evil regimes.

Along the path, God continually asserted kingship over the children of Abraham. Part of God's message promised a Messiah, a Spirit-anointed Savior for God's people of faith. Isaiah declared this Messiah's miraculous conception and birth in these prophecies:

For to us a child is born, to us a son is given, and the government will be on his shoulders. And he will be called Wonderful Counselor, the Mighty God, Everlasting Father, Prince of Peace. [87]

The virgin will conceive and give birth to a son, and will call him Immanuel. [88]

Finally, the first Christmas Day arrived and Jesus Christ was born. God's promises began to find their rich fulfillment!

THE HOLY SPIRIT'S ROLE

As John the Baptist declared just before the onset of Jesus' public ministry, the coming of the Christ meant the kingdom of God was at hand. [89] Let's remember that the word *Christ* (Greek) or *messiah* (Hebrew) both mean "the anointed one." The title promised more than just an oily unction poured ceremoniously on the head and oozing down the shoulders of some hereditary king or chosen prophet. Rather, it promised that the coming Savior would come in the power of the Spirit of God. The Spirit would anoint Him to perform His task.

John the Baptist declared the kingdom's arrival. He said, "I baptize with water, but the one who is coming is stronger than I. He will baptize with the Holy Spirit." [90] All four Gospels record John's proclamation that the Spirit will powerfully anoint the Messiah. But He will also powerfully anoint *all* of God's people with that same Spirit. The phrase John used, "baptism in the Spirit" was a brand new metaphor. It probably shocked his first listeners, and remains a controversial phrase among Christians to this day. Perhaps for that reason the phrase was virtually ignored for most of the church's history. But for John, baptism in the Spirit marked out the true distinguishing ministry of the Messiah. No other prophet had ever had such an anointing to anoint others. Jesus would be the ultimate "man of the Spirit."

> **FOR JOHN, BAPTISM IN THE SPIRIT MARKED OUT THE TRUE DISTINGUISHING MINISTRY OF THE MESSIAH.**

John's declaration of Jesus' unique role as Spirit-baptizer provides a foundational understanding for the kingdom of God. John knew that the fulfillment of the prophecy in Joel 2:28 would mark the arrival of the kingdom: "I will pour out my Spirit on all people." The kingdom could not arrive until God fulfilled Joel's prophecy—and the Lord richly fulfilled John's prophecy on the day of Pentecost. On that day, Jesus filled the church with the Holy Spirit. Only after Pentecost could the church *fully* take up its kingdom mission. [91] And God revealed that mission to the disciples only after Jesus died on the cross and rose from the dead.

THE CHURCH'S COMMISSION

Jesus trained His disciples in many aspects of the kingdom before His death. But He didn't reveal their *commission* until after He had made *remission* for sins on the cross. The kingdom of God couldn't rule in the hearts of men and women until Jesus had reconciled God and humanity through the cross. Any declaration of the kingdom of God among men and women today that excludes the cross of Christ rings false.

As a child, I remember seeing a poster at the county fair in which someone provocatively claimed that Psalm 14:1 says, "There is no God." Upon looking up the verse, you find that it actually says, "The fool says in his heart, 'There is no God.'" Unless you read the whole verse, the statement lies. Similarly, any statement of the kingdom that leaves out the cross also lies.

Once Jesus had completed His work on the cross, He revealed the mission of the church. To the small group of disciples who remained, He declared His full control of the kingdom of God. "All authority in heaven and on earth has been given to me." [92] The cross and the resurrection guaranteed the King's presence and also certified that His Father had fully vested Him with kingdom authority. Working in that kingly authority, Jesus gave His disciples the Great Commission:

> Therefore go and make disciples of all nations, baptizing them in the name of the Father and of the Son and of the Holy Spirit, and teaching them to obey everything I have commanded you. And surely I am with you always, to the very end of the age. [93]

That commission is the mission of the church.

Through this commission, the church not only enters a mission to redeem humanity, but also to redeem the mission of humanity. Notice the striking parallels between the two missions.

Genesis 1:28 records God's command to human beings to multiply, migrate, and rule. Likewise, Jesus commands the church to migrate (go into all nations, thus scattering around the world), to multiply (make disciples and baptize them in Trinitarian authority), and to rule (or "take dominion") for Christ (teach them to obey everything He had commanded). [94] So, the mission of the church redeems all three parts of the mission of humanity.

Back in the 1920s, an episode known as the Fundamentalist-Modernist Controversy led to a disaster for Christianity. After the public scandal of the so-called Scopes Monkey Trial and the resulting loss of favor in American society of conservative churches, many Christians decided to pull away from society and gather in sectarian groups. [95] It almost seemed they understood the Great Commission to mean, "Go into the world. Gather people into congregations. Teach them a fortress mentality. And help them hide out until I come back."

> **THE MISSION OF THE CHURCH REDEEMS ALL THREE PARTS OF THE MISSION OF HUMANITY.**

Fortunately, leaders like Carl F. H. Henry and Billy Graham led evangelicals to re-engage with society after World War II. The Great Commission, they understood, has far more exciting and world-embracing implications than the fundamentalists had understood. Jesus meant for the Great Commission both to redeem our earthly life *and* to salvage our earthly mission.

In God's plan to salvage our mission, God's reign on earth stands against the rule of injustice and evil. Ponder Jesus' teaching about the kingdom of God in the Beatitudes. He called "blessed" or "happy" the poor, the mourners, the meek, the merciful, the peacemakers, the hungry, the thirsty, and those persecuted for righteousness. Their happiness comes from the fact that the coming kingdom will set all their troubles right and will fulfill all their longings. Because these "blessed ones" get glimpses into the conditions of the kingdom, they think the announcement of the kingdom has credibility. Jesus told a discouraged John the Baptist that, "The blind receive sight, the lame walk, those who have leprosy are cleansed, the deaf hear, the dead are raised, and the good news is proclaimed to the poor." [96] These miracles provided glimpses of the conditions of the kingdom of heaven.

By the power of the Spirit, the proclamation of the good news still includes all of those elements. Christian people walk through life in obedience to the Word of God, fulfilling the human mission. Having children, filling the earth, building cultures structured and colored by the values of the kingdom, fighting injustice in the name of the all-righteous God—all those things constitute obedience to Jesus and the fulfillment of the church's commission.

Of course, no human culture can ever perfectly represent the kingdom of God. The kingdom will not manifest itself completely in the world until King Jesus returns to fulfill the human and Christian missions. (Perhaps that success will occur mostly in spite of us, not so much because of us.) When He comes, He will heroically achieve our final success by utterly crushing the kingdom of darkness.

BUILDING THE KINGDOM?

We must never believe that our good works "build the kingdom," for that common phrase has a big problem. The New Testament *never* tells us to build the kingdom. Rather, God calls us to *proclaim* the kingdom. Only Jesus can "build the kingdom."

But even if we cannot build the kingdom, the kingdom networks woven by Jesus' followers can provide the means for Him to build His kingdom by the power of the Holy Spirit in the world. Human obedience can illustrate to humanity the reality of God's kingdom; our works and our cultures should provide glimpses of the kingdom of heaven.

I love the words of the patriotic hymn, "America the Beautiful." I especially love the stanza that says, "Oh beautiful for patriot dream/ that sees beyond the years/ thine alabaster cities gleam/ undimmed by human tears." [97] That verse reminds us of our Pilgrim and Puritan ancestors. In response to Jesus' Beatitudes sermon, they conceived of America as a "city set on a hill." [98] They intended to build a society true to the values of the kingdom. Basing their society on biblical laws and biblical principles, they sought to become full-on disciples, obeying the commands of Jesus in all things. They sought to make their country an embassy of heaven.

As a missionary living overseas, I used to love doing business at the United States Embassy. Stepping into an American embassy means stepping onto American soil—where the laws of the host country do not apply, but rather, the laws of America. Ideally (though not always in practice), the embassy speaks American English. It observes American customs. It represents American interests. It is America writ tiny.

As one of the great privileges of my life, I officiated at the wedding of my daughter, Jessica. I encouraged her and her husband, Nathan, to make their home an embassy of heaven. Christian homes should observe the customs, laws, and interests of the kingdom of God, to the greatest degree we can achieve. The pilgrims saw America as an embassy of the kingdom of heaven in the world. They strove to establish the values of the kingdom as American values. They sought to obey the commands of Jesus through the laws of the land. They worked to provide glimpses into the realities of heaven's Sabbath in the midst of the work-a-day world.

Did they fail? We have the alabaster cities the hymn mentions. No society in human history has ever achieved the wealth and comforts that the American Pilgrim's dream has provided. (Don't confuse the Pilgrim's dream with the current, more secularized version of the American Dream). But the alabaster cities' gleam has never gone "undimmed by human tears." America's cities still carry the tarnish of tearstains, still fouled by the fall. So did the Pilgrims fail?

> **THE KINGDOM NETWORKS WOVEN BY JESUS' FOLLOWERS CAN PROVIDE THE MEANS FOR HIM TO BUILD HIS KINGDOM BY THE POWER OF THE HOLY SPIRIT.**

I would insist they did not. America's future deeply concerns me, as we move farther and farther into a godless and secular model of society. The Pilgrims' vision may grow dimmer and dimmer in the years to come. Or a great spiritual awakening may even now dawn in America. None of us knows the future. But I know that the Pilgrims' efforts to obey God and reflect God's kingdom in our society provided key elements in America's historical greatness. The ugly parts of our history—terrible things such as slavery and imperialism—made up no part of their dream, but rather came from competing versions of the American Dream. We don't get the privilege of weaving the kingdom net without interference! Nor do we get to work the net in unspoiled waters. The net catches both good fish and bad. But the work of the kingdom net nevertheless yields its catch. We will do better working with the net than without it.

Does even the most secular person in America scoff at the nobility of the Pilgrims' dream? An objective judge who looked at the history of our nation would deem it one of the greatest experiments in human governance and culture the world has ever witnessed. Not many countries in the world today do a better job of providing freedom and justice through governance, and all countries owe some measure of debt to American ideals and examples. Our system has succeeded because so many of our founders and their followers actively sought to reflect the kingdom of God in our society.

Let's be clear. America is not the kingdom of God—far from it. But it draws closer to it when God's people believe that their efforts to live according to the values of the kingdom can have a positive effect in the world and leave strong evidence of the kingdom in it. In due time, every nation in the world will become "the kingdom of our Lord and of his Messiah." [99] But until the mission of the church has finished its objective and the mission of humanity has fulfilled its end, the kingdom will continue to be "already and not yet." Jesus will indeed return to claim and establish His throne in the world.

Until Jesus comes again, the church has a redemptive mission to pursue. We cannot *build* the kingdom. But we can proclaim the good news of the kingdom in the power of the Holy Spirit, reconciling people to God through the preaching of the cross. Our mission as humans requires us to do more than evangelize the world. But our mission as members of the church requires us to achieve no less than the clear proclamation of Jesus as Lord.

THE CO-MISSION

When we proclaim the Lordship of Jesus explicitly through our words and by living out Christian discipleship through faithful execution of the human mission, we fulfill the Great Commission. We cannot do the job alone in either of these crucial elements of the task. The kingdom net requires that we live out our mission in community with other people, both believers in Christ and unbelievers. If our personal networks become too congregational— all focused on the church and its interior life—we can fully accomplish neither proclamation nor discipleship. Likewise, if we don't tie ourselves into a community of believers, we fail to obey all that the Word of God has commanded us to do. *Commitment to the commission requires us to be in communion.*

> **UNTIL JESUS COMES AGAIN, THE CHURCH HAS A REDEMPTIVE MISSION TO PURSUE.**

So the Great Commission requires us to declare the good news of the kingdom through the reconciliation brought by the cross. It requires us to lean not on our own strength, but to get our power from the Holy Spirit, who baptizes us into Christ when we are born again. It also requires us to restore the fullness of the human mission through walking with God in Christian discipleship and obedience to the Word of Christ. And it is a worldwide mission through which every nation, people, tongue, and tribe can hear the good news so they, in turn, may go out to reach others.

All of that requires some impressive networking!

WORKING THE NET

The Great Commission is a fishing enterprise that deploys the kingdom net.

1. Who were some of the people God used to proclaim the kingdom to you? Do you know who influenced them to submit to the rule of King Jesus? If they are still living, take time to write and send a thank-you note to three of them and let them know what God is doing in your life now.

2. Who are the top five people in your life who need to enter the kingdom? Put them on your regular prayer list, and take time now to pray for them and to ask God to work them into the kingdom net. You may not be the ideal person to bring them to Jesus, but you are an ideal person to pray for them. Ask God to put other kingdom networkers in their path who will be able to lead them to the Lord. If you've never shared your faith with them, ask God for golden opportunities to share.

3. List three ways you're working with other believers to proclaim the kingdom. If you can't come up with three ways, start praying about how you can be more involved in connecting other people to God.

CHAPTER EIGHT

▶ IMITATE ◀

PAUL THE NETWORKER

T he apostle Paul was one of the greatest networkers in the history of the kingdom. While he didn't follow Jesus during the Lord's flesh-and-blood presence on earth, Paul mastered the art of networking, just like Jesus did. Paul's story will enlighten anyone who wants to understand the networking principles that Jesus used.

Paul's life began in the city of Tarsus, an important Roman imperial capital in what we know as Turkey. [100] Speaking Greek as his first language, as his writings make clear, Paul had received an excellent education in Greek and Roman philosophy and literature. He came from a wealthy Jewish family, and at some time during his youth, his strong Jewish piety led him to emigrate to Jerusalem. Through his strong networking skills, he managed to become a disciple of the great Rabbi Gamaliel, one of Judaism's greatest religious authorities and a prominent member of the Jewish High Court, the Sanhedrin. [101]

Paul describes himself as "advancing rapidly in Judaism" at the time of his conversion. [102] Like any upwardly mobile leader, he knew how to turn contacts into relationships that would advance his career. When the Bible first mentions him, he had already become either a member or powerful agent of the Sanhedrin. Like a lot of corporate leaders today, he would willingly step on others in order to secure his own advancement. The evangelist Stephen became the first victim of his ambition. [103] Using his relationship with the Jewish high priest, Paul subsequently got letters of introduction to synagogues in Damascus that would allow him to arrest Christians there and bring them back to Jerusalem for trial and punishment.

Along with a group of associates, Paul traveled to Damascus—and on the way there, he encountered the Way, Jesus Christ Himself. (His encounter with the Way soon resulted in an encounter with the highway, as he fell to the ground, blinded by the divine glory that radiated from Jesus.) At that point, Paul got caught up in the kingdom net.

Before he met Jesus, Paul worked his own net, sought his own advancement, and went off (truly "off") on his own mission. After meeting Jesus, he quickly went from Wrong Way to Straight Street. [104] As Paul adopted a posture of obedience, Jesus showed him a vision of a man named Ananias. Jesus, the consummate networker, also appeared to Ananias in a vision and introduced him to Paul. As Paul and Ananias got together, Paul received healing and the infilling of the Holy Spirit.

THE BEGINNINGS OF PAUL'S NETWORK

Networking usually involves a process much like this: A friend introduces you to someone, either personally or through letters, emails, phone calls, or other means (though not often through a miraculous vision!). You set up a meeting with that person, and you get to know each other. If the meeting succeeds, and if you both see your purposes as complementary, that meeting may become an ongoing relationship. Often at that first meeting, you share additional contacts and arrange more meetings. The network of relationships, and often professional collaboration or business interactions, gets bigger and more profitable.

Something like that happened to Paul. Just hours previously, the two men had been mortal enemies. But Ananias and Paul established a strong connection at their first meeting (with a lot of help from Jesus and the Holy Spirit). We have no better victories in all our networking than those that occur when former enemies, competitors, or rivals find common ground and new futures together! Smart professionals stay as relationally close to their competitors as possible. Just today, I read a headline in the *Seattle Times* about a friendly encounter between the CEOs of Apple and Microsoft. As a college president, I not only seek to spend time with presidents from competing institutions, but I also keep some of the closest ones on my prayer list.

Ananias opened up his network to Paul, and soon Paul began to add new contacts to both of their networks. In time, he returned to Jerusalem to meet the original apostles of Jesus, who understandably declined to trust him because of his deadly reputation. Nevertheless, he established a relationship with Joseph Barnabas, one of the church's earliest financial benefactors. [105] Money talks, and the large donor convinced the senior leaders of the kingdom net to weave Paul into their network. Immediately, Paul put his skills to work sharing the gospel—so effectively that his former associates, foreign-born Jews like himself called the Hellenists, tried to kill him. As a result, he had to flee to Antioch, along with his new associate, Joseph Barnabas.

In Antioch, Paul and Barnabas quickly established a multicultural network of prophets and teachers, and through their efforts, the kingdom net spread wider and wider. [106] That group included a black man named Simeon, a Cyrenian named Lucius, and Manaen, a member of the royal court of Herod. I find it remarkable how Paul, in every place he set out to establish the kingdom net, managed to establish relationships with talented people from a broad range of backgrounds and talents. Long before the twenty-first century practice of seeking strength through diversity became the rage, Paul understood that a multinational organization needed diversity to succeed.

Before long, the church in Antioch obeyed the direction of the Holy Spirit to send Paul and Barnabas on a series of missionary journeys in order to expand the network. In their first stop, on the Island of Cyprus, they quickly established a network that allowed them to meet personally with the Roman proconsul, Sergius Paulus, whom Acts 13:7 refers to as "an intelligent man." Not only did he and Paul share a name, they shared a similar background as Roman citizens and as men trained in the Greco-Roman system of education. Paul managed to appeal not only to the proconsul's mind, but when harshly challenged by Elymas the magician—one of Sergius Paulus' associates—he struck the opponent blind by the power of the Holy Spirit. The incident confirmed the proconsul's nascent faith, and as the highest-ranking Roman official on the island, he no doubt served as an invaluable resource for the kingdom net.

Even in this brief recounting of Paul's networking, we see that the apostle loved to establish relationships with highly significant leaders. The rest of his career would show that he pushed and pushed until he had a personal audience with Caesar himself. His story also reveals that he willingly associated closely with slaves and so-called ordinary people. Don't miss the point here! Your networking needs to include people from all social levels. It doesn't matter whether you work in the church, in business, or in politics, professional practice, or any other sphere. There is no such thing as a useless person or a useless relationship.

According to research conducted by Stanley Milgram in the 1950s and '60s, people in the United States are separated by only three friendship links. [107] (A popular "small world" theory suggests that no more than six degrees of separation divide everyone in the world.) Amazingly, only two or three friendships probably separate you from a person you need to meet, who could help you make serious progress on some current project. You never know who will be the key to opening up your access to the people you need to know the most.

Throughout his career, Paul built a huge network of friends and colleagues and co-laborers. To finance his missionary efforts (and perhaps as importantly, to open up new contacts for the kingdom net in the business communities of the Roman world), he operated a tent-making enterprise. The same networking skills that made him an effective evangelist and church planter also made him an excellent businessman. Two of his associates in the double enterprise of tent-making and net weaving were Aquila and Priscilla (also known as Priscilla and Aquila, a highly talented couple who seemed to enjoy an egalitarian relationship).

Originally from Pontus, a region on the Black Sea in modern-day Turkey, Aquila worked as a truly international businessman. [108]

Before meeting Paul in Corinth (Greece), he and Priscilla lived in Rome. As Jewish Christians and leaders in the Roman churches, they had gotten caught up in a controversy among Jews and, along with all the other Jews, got evicted from the so-called Eternal City by the emperor himself. Paul went to see them, and this brilliant piece of networking resulted in their doing business together. [109] This relationship would later prove beneficial in many ways as Paul continued to work the kingdom net.

THE EPISTLE TO THE ROMANS

We see Paul's networking method clearly in his letter to the churches of Rome. The letter to the Romans is in itself a remarkable piece of networking. Unlike the other cities to which Paul sent letters, the apostle didn't found the Roman church and apparently had never visited Rome during his Christian life.

As he began his letter, he made it plain that he wanted to visit the Romans and to "reap some harvest" among them. [110] Undoubtedly, Paul wished to reap some harvest in the way Christians usually mean that term, i.e., in the sense of winning new converts to faith in Christ. But he also made clear that he wanted to reap some monetary harvest. He announced his hope to see them in passing as he traveled to Spain, and to receive "help" on his journey from them. [111] He mentioned his journey to Jerusalem to deliver a love offering he had received from the churches in Macedonia and Achaia (hint, hint). Imagine—at least part of the motivation for the great theological treatise that is the epistle to the Romans was *fundraising!*

If you've carefully studied the book of Romans, you may have noticed its double ending. Paul finished the book in 15:33

with a prayer for peace and his amen, and yet in the next verse, he started up again, commending Phoebe to the Romans. What was going on there?

In fact, Romans 16:1ff is a letter of reference that certified Phoebe, as the carrier of the letter, to the Romans. They would have read that letter first, not last; we could regard it as the true first chapter of the book of Romans. In that recommendation letter—a well-established custom of networkers throughout history and one that takes up a fair amount of my time as a university president—Paul tried not only to establish Phoebe's credentials, but also to burnish his own. Let's take a look at the network Paul laid out in his attempt to include the Roman churches in his network.

He first mentioned Priscilla and Aquila, his old business partners from Corinth who had returned to Rome to lead a prominent house church. Claudius had taken over from Nero, taking the heat off for Jews, and for years many Jews had begun filtering back into the city. Whether for business or evangelistic purposes, Priscilla and Aquila had also returned to Rome and likely had become the most important leaders among the churches there. Paul accordingly mentioned them first, pointing out that they had risked their lives for him in Corinth, a distinction that outranks mere business partners. Paul knew that as the Roman churches respected Priscilla and Aquila they would respect him as a close friend of theirs.

Undoubtedly, the lack of detail in his dramatic announcement would result in Priscilla and Aquila having to explain the matter to those around them, making them the heroes of stories in which he played a prominent role.

NETWORKING TIP

*Make other people the heroes of your stories and you'll get more
networking benefit than you would by tooting your own horn.*

If you can put your associates in the position of telling positive
stories about how they have helped you, you will do well. In many
cases, they'll make you the hero of the story to avoid seeming too
proud. They may explain why they went out of their way to help
you, testifying to your prestige far more persuasively than you could
do for yourself.

Does this idea sound manipulative or Machiavellian to you?
Remember that you must never speak insincerely or falsely in any
way. If you make yourself the star of every story you tell, you'll
never become an effective networker, for nobody trusts or even
likes a braggart. Being a phony will deep-six your networking. The
French diplomat Jean Giraudoux famously said that "the secret of
success is sincerity; once you can fake that, you've got it made." [112]
Don't believe it. Sincerity is the coin of the realm in networking,
and influential people can pick out a phony a mile away.

Paul then mentioned his friend Epaenetus, the first convert
to Christ in Asia, the Roman name for what we call Turkey. In
mentioning him, Paul not only established the prestige of Epaenetus,
but also the fact that he himself was among the first to preach in
Asia. Epaenetus would also receive some well-deserved recognition
as people heard of his pioneering role in the establishment of
Christian faith around the world. While I doubt that Paul saw this
as a "technique," it certainly is an effective one.

Establishing your relationship to the founders of any institution lends you a certain authority to interpret that institution.

Whether on purpose or by great networking instincts, Paul went to great lengths to establish his seniority in the kingdom. He mentioned Mary, who needed no last name or further description. The Roman church knew her well, and she could have been one of the several women named Mary whom Jesus counted as close friends. Mary the mother of John Mark qualifies as a possible candidate. Paul also mentioned Andronicus and Junia, referring to them as his "kinfolk" and mentioning that the apostles knew them well and that they were "in Christ" before him. As before, these cryptic references provided another opportunity for these Christian pioneers to tell their stories and describe how they got to know Paul. As Paul's relatives, Andronicus and Junia no doubt felt proud of his service to Christ and so eagerly told his story in a way that modesty would have prevented the apostle himself from doing. "Blood is thicker than water," and the recommendation of a trusted family member adds inestimable value in building your network.

NETWORKING TIP

While nobody likes nepotism, family relationships are golden for networking.

The next few names in Paul's list of friends might seem counterintuitive to people who want to make the most of their relationships for networking. He listed Ampliatus, Apelles, Urbanus, and Stachys as beloved coworkers "approved in Christ." We don't know who they were, because to history, they are nobodies. We do know that slaves in Caesar's household commonly had those names, and having no better theory for identifying them, we may assume that Paul mentioned them because of that relationship. We know that later on Paul had friends in Caesar's "household" (i.e., among Caesar's slaves), because he mentioned them in Philippians 4:21.

The likelihood that these friends of Paul belonged to the imperial household increases by another contact he mentioned, the household of Aristobulus. It is "highly probable," according to the great Romans scholar C. E. B. Cranfield, that Aristobulus was the grandson of King Herod the Great, the brother of Herod Agrippa I. [113] Though probably not a Christian, he figured among the well-known and wealthy residents of Rome. His royal background would give the position of his slaves a similar status to those of Caesar's household.

The next person mentioned is Herodion (or "Little Herod"), a Jewish Christian whose name "naturally suggests a connection (probably a slave or freedman) of the Herod family." [114] It seems likely he was a leading member of the household, since Paul singled him out. By mentioning slaves and possibly freedmen in the households of Caesar and Aristobulus, Paul gained a paradoxical double-yield: he not only considered these slaves his beloved colleagues, demonstrating his humility and his habit of valuing people without respect to their social class, but he also gained the prestige of the imperial household.

In fact, humble people in the service of powerful people have huge potential power. They can really help you, so they doubly deserve your respect! They deserve respect for their own personal value as well as for the value of the prestigious boss they serve. Bosses like to see others treat their people with respect. When a person treats my employees with disrespect, I usually take it either as an insult to me or as an indication of the person's poor judgment.

NETWORKING TIP

Treat the employees of people you want to meet with the same respect you hold for their boss.

If you treat the employees of the people you want to influence with the respect they deserve, they will open doors for you. They also will speak well of you to others. In the case of the Roman church, Paul could certainly expect the imperial slaves to speak well of him, especially after he had spoken so well of them. Later on, they would continue to count themselves his faithful friends, not only when he came to visit, but when he wound up living in Rome under house arrest (Acts 28).

Paul then mentioned the household of Narcissus, a famous and wealthy former slave granted his freedom by Emperor Tiberius. [115] The mention of this notable freedman in the context of greeting the slaves of Caesar and Aristobulus serves as an interesting reminder of what a slave can become. Members of the church who didn't feel impressed with Paul's close relationships with the slaves of the wealthy and powerful thus got a reminder that such people can rise to great heights.

Today's mailroom clerk may become tomorrow's CEO. Never judge a person's future power on the basis of their current position.

Paul also sent greetings to Tryphena and Tryphosa, most likely twins, since in Roman times twins often received similar sounding names. Paul called these women "hard workers." Regardless of your networking goal, make it a priority to create friendships with hard-working people. Paul also added a greeting to Persis, yet another hard worker.

NETWORKING TIP

Pay special attention to hard workers. Hard work is the key to all professional success, and everyone respects people who work hard.

As Paul continued his networking *tour de force,* he greeted Rufus and his mother. Notice that Rufus needed no introduction. He was probably the same Rufus mentioned in the gospel of Mark (a book written to the Roman church), one of the sons of Simon of Cyrene. [116] Simon, you may remember, got pressed into duty to carry the cross when Jesus became too weak to continue up the hill to Golgotha. It's hard to imagine a greater dignity to pass on to one's children.

Rufus would have had an extremely important voice in the church. Either he was an eyewitness of the crucifixion (and the resurrection!) or he was the son of an eyewitness. He may have been present at Pentecost, or among the Cyrenians mentioned in Acts 2 who heard the mysteries of God declared in their own language. At any rate, he likely enjoyed considerable fame among the believers.

Firmly resist the impulse to cultivate famous people for selfish motives. Befriend them because they, like you, need sincere friends. Kingdom networking always seeks to serve those whom God has already worked into the net. It also seeks to activate one's own service to others. By the way, don't fool yourself. Famous people can see through "users" immediately. People try to take advantage of them all the time; that's why you need to come to them with absolute sincerity.

NETWORKING TIP

You can't get to know enough famous people. Having famous friends opens up connections to their many friends.

History doesn't remember the next series of ten people to whom Paul sent greetings. Even Paul may not have known them personally, since he added no biographical details and the greetings seem fairly routine. It does seem interesting that he mentioned "all the saints who are with them." We can reasonably assume they were all house-church leaders, since they represent other brothers and sisters. This idea finds support in the next phrase, which asks them all to greet each other with a kiss and includes his greetings from "all the churches of Christ."

It's a good thing to send greetings to people you don't know through people you do know.

GREETINGS FROM CORINTH

As Paul finished mentioning and greeting his friends in the Roman church, he went on to mention friends with him in Corinth. He expected their identities would have meaning to the new friends he wanted to make in Rome. He first mentioned Timothy, known throughout the Christian world as Paul's protégé.

In that same section, Paul also mentioned his secretary, Tertius, who took dictation from the apostle in writing down the book.

Take care to speak well of your secretary or administrative assistant or chief of staff. If they look good, you look good. If they look bad, you look even worse for having such an incompetent person work for you. My assistants always make me look good, and I try never to make them look bad. This often means people feel just as happy to meet them as they are to meet me. I felt tickled one day when an important person I had befriended said to me with delight, "I got to meet Dani today!" Dani Haynes had set up our meetings with such charm that he looked forward to meeting her. I promoted Dani from

Executive Assistant to Director of Event Relations, but I often get the same kinds of comments about my current administrative assistants, Polly Reasner and Anne Kuchera, and my student assistants. Of course, I always feel proud to have such capable people representing me. A great staff is networking gold!

NETWORKING TIP

*Make the people who work under your authority—
especially those who act in your authority—look good.*

Paul also mentioned Lucius, Jason, and Sosipater, his "kinsmen." By kinsmen, he may have meant no more than that they were all Jews. We don't know the identity of Lucius, but it seems likely he's the same person mentioned in Acts 17:5–7, 9. We see Paul's relationship with Jason in the words of a mob in Thessalonica, who angrily said of Paul and his companions: "These men who have caused trouble all over the world have now come here, and Jason has welcomed them into his house." [117] Sosipater is probably the same person as Sopater from Berea, a traveling companion and "advance man" of Paul mentioned in Acts 20:4. Both of these Macedonians had begun their ministry by serving Paul. [118] But apparently, their traveling ministry for the gospel had made them known to the believers in Rome, who probably knew them better than they did the apostle himself, since he had never visited the Roman churches. Both had been disciples and companions of Paul, whose ministry had blessed others.

Jason and Sosipater illustrate the principle that you can have no better networking contacts than the people you've had a role in developing. Whether in church ministry or in secular professions, people who have benefited from your tutelage can aid you in building your network.

NETWORKING TIP

People who respect your disciples and protégés will typically have automatic respect for you, based on the stories they have heard about you.

Paul goes on to mention Gaius, his host in Corinth, the same wealthy man mentioned in 1 Corinthians 1:14 who owned a home large enough to accommodate the whole church. Wealthy people have the same inherent human value as everyone else, but wealthy people almost always have real talents that helped them either to earn or maintain their wealth. Boards of directors at Christian institutions usually seek wealthy people as members, and not just because they can make large gifts to fund the work. Wealthy people tend to have a lot of wisdom, know-how, and psychological health and maturity.

NETWORKING TIP

In building your personal network and weaving it into the kingdom, it's foolish not to take wealthy people seriously.

Believers see classism, like racism or sexism, as a truly ugly "ism." But people in the church often don't recognize an active prejudice against rich people. In one church I attended, I knew a couple in which the husband looked up to rich people, while the wife looked askance at them. Accordingly, they didn't see eye-to-eye on the topic. The woman grew up in sooty, coal-mining poverty and always felt that rich people looked down on her. She responded by judging rich people negatively, even as she fantasized about becoming wealthy herself. The man, on the other hand, grew up in the dirt-poor world of tenant farming. He recognized the rich people he knew as hard workers and smart, and that most of them had earned their position in life. He wanted to become as much like them as possible: working hard, being smart, cutting a good figure in society, and trying to achieve as much as he could. The husband had the right idea and he prospered in his career, despite his wife's discomfort around financially successful people.

You don't have to treat wealthy or powerful people with exaggerated courtesy. Most of them just want to be treated like everyone else. But it is both foolish and sinful to envy the wealth of others, and it makes no sense at all professionally to alienate wealthy people. Classism errs in all directions, especially in the kingdom net where only Jesus stands above us *and* at the center.

Finally, Paul included a greeting from Erastus, a powerful government official in Corinth, and Quartus. Erastus, mentioned in Acts 19:22 and 2 Timothy 4:20, served as the city treasurer in Corinth. To this day, a limestone pavement near the theater in Corinth has an inscription in Latin from Paul's time that states: "Erastus in return for his [government position] laid [this pavement] at his own expense." This Erastus may well be the same man Paul mentions. [119] If so, the inscription portrays Erastus as both powerful and wealthy. His association with Quartus suggests the same, since Quartus is Greek for "Thurston Howell the Third." [120] (Just kidding! Literally, the name means "fourth," suggesting that he was either the fourth person of a certain name in his family, or more likely, the fourth child in the family. Romans often gave slaves born in their households such names—First, Second, Third, etc.).

When you make friends with people who know a lot of people, you strike a rich lode of gold ore to mine for your networks.

NETWORKING TIP

People who hold positions of power in government or business or professional agencies or the like are extremely important nodes in your network. They can be of incredible value in opening doors for you to carry out God's calling on your life.

PAUL'S EXAMPLE

Paul had many friends who themselves had many other friends. Romans 16 illustrates so richly that Paul knew how to make the most of his relationships to fulfill his calling. He knew that the kingdom could not spread through the work of preachers alone. He had a unique calling as the Apostle to the Nations (Gentiles). But he could never have accomplished it without the help of family members, servants, employees, volunteers, hard workers, professionals such as Luke the physician, people of high and low social position, famous people, rich and successful people, and powerful allies. Since the kingdom is a social network, it requires people and relationships if it is to survive and thrive in the world.

Paul succeeded in his mission of planting new churches and expanding the network of believers in Jesus throughout the Gentile world. He said, "Follow my example, as I follow the example of Christ." [121] We can all benefit by following Paul's example and making the most of our own relationships.

Your relationships can create synergies and systems and new ventures that will proclaim the gospel of the kingdom to men and women around the world, just as Paul's did. Regardless of what area of work your gifts make ideal for you, your truest calling is to follow Jesus, the Master Networker, in making the kingdom known as widely as possible.

WORKING THE NET

1. In the table below, fill in the blanks with the name of a person you know who fits the description. Also indicate whether you fit that description yourself.

Description	Example	Do you fit?
Often tells stories in which other people are the heroes		
Knows a lot about the founding of the organization he or she works for		
Effectively makes use of family relationships		
Treats the employees of other people with the same respect he or she has for the boss		
Is a hard worker		
Often sends greetings to people		
Knows a few famous people		

Makes people who work under their authority look good		
Knows how to get along with wealthy people		
Has a position of authority in government, business, or ministry		

If you found that you fit any of those descriptions, it means that you would be a good person for others to know. Feel good about networking with others and sharing your wisdom with them.

If you didn't fit one or more of the descriptions above, make a point of calling (or calling on) the person whose name you wrote in the corresponding box. Pay them a compliment by saying, "I was reading *The Kingdom Net,* a book about networking, and I thought of you as an example of a person who is good at (fill in the blank)." Tell them you admire their skill and ask them to give you some advice that would help you improve. Be tactful. Don't say anything like, "I noticed that you're really good at using your family to get ahead."

CHAPTER NINE

DO

NAME-DROPPING DOS AND DON'TS

D o you hate name-droppers? A lot of people do. And yet, one of the most powerful instruments known to networkers is the art of name-dropping. You must absolutely master this dangerous catch-22, or you will bring negative consequences on yourself and your reputation. Alternatively, you will fail to connect to people in a powerful way that can pay enormous rewards to both you and them. To paraphrase Rowlf the dog in *The Muppet Movie,* you "can't live with it, can't live without it." [122] You really must learn how to artfully drop names if you want to become a successful networker.

Why do people hate name-droppers? It's simple. Nobody likes someone who's always bragging about the famous people they know. It sounds pretentious and arrogant, and as everyone knows, usually it's phony. Those who really *do* know lots of celebrities and famous people have no intention of telling everyone about it. Famous and powerful people like to keep their privacy as much as possible, and when they discern that they can't trust certain people to keep their mouths shut about being their friends, they cut them off. They develop a sixth sense about such things, and they don't let those kinds of people get close to them.

People who constantly brag about who they know are usually trying to make themselves look important and impress others. The quickest way to fail at impressing others is to try to make them feel "less than" (<) while holding yourself out as "greater than" (>). In networking, you look for parallel relationships (=). Expressed as a mathematical formula, we could explain it like this: $> = <$. Get it? When you look for an even-steven relationship, don't accept the less-than/greater-than concept. Don't even grasp for equality. Rather, treat people as if they were more important than you, even if you outrank the person you're trying to engage.[123] Rank ≠ superiority. If you treat people as greater than yourself, they'll rightly appreciate you as humble, and they'll love you for it. By treating others as greater than yourself, you'll establish yourself as anyone's equal.

Based on this principle of "name-dropping for equality," try to observe the following rules in dropping names:

NEVER DROP A NAME WHEN . . .

1. you doubt that your potential friend will have a personal relationship with the person whose name you intend to mention;
2. you don't really know the person whose name you are dropping;
3. the person is the most famous person in the organization your potential friend belongs to;

4. the person greatly outranks your potential friend.

So in these cases, what can you do instead of name-dropping? You don't have to know a person to drop their name. You could say, "Oh, I've greatly admired your boss, Bill Gates. Have you ever met him personally?" That gives the new acquaintance a chance to either brag about their association with that person or confess that they, too, have admired the eminent colleague from afar. If they haven't met the person, refrain from stating that you have. Consider, however, that people at Microsoft or the Gates Foundation have heard that line about ten million times and may not feel thrilled to hear it again. That's especially true if they haven't met the Great Eminence; better in such a case to mention some other person than the most famous member of that organization.

> **WHY IS NAME-DROPPING IMPORTANT? BECAUSE NETWORKS ARE ALL ABOUT PEOPLE!**

ALWAYS DROP A NAME WHEN . . .

1. you actually have a friend in the organization or association and you think the person also may know that individual;
2. you can make them feel special by letting them talk about their relationship with the name you intend to drop.

Why is name-dropping important? Because networks are all about people! If you can establish that you have a mutual acquaintance, it offers you instant legitimacy. It provides a powerful starting place for meaningful conversation that builds a sense of trust. It can also build things like a sense of shared suffering (if perhaps you shared a tough professor or a bad boss). It also clearly positions you as a potential colleague who belongs in their network because you already have a connection to an existing "node."

BEFRIENDING THE SECRETARY

A particularly powerful but sometimes overlooked category in the name-dropping game is the name of a secretary, personal assistant, or administrative assistant. As Paul demonstrated in Romans, the servants of powerful people have real power themselves. Never, *ever* treat a secretary or assistant as if they were one bit less important than their boss.

Earlier in my career, when I served as a missionary to Latin America, I had to raise my own salary by visiting lots of American churches, preaching to or greeting the congregation, and then presenting a case for their making a monthly pledge of support to my ministry. In order to arrange such opportunities, I had to get on the telephone and call pastors. I often knew absolutely nothing about the churches I called, except that they were listed in our denominational directory. Would you believe that such a task feels a little daunting?

I always felt happy to visit any church, large or small. I occasionally got a large pledge or offering from small churches, and I occasionally got either no pledge or a shockingly small offering from very large churches. Like Forrest Gump's mother used to say about boxes of chocolate, you never knew what you were going to get. [124] But I always considered it a great privilege to speak to any church of any size, and I always trusted that God would take care of my needs if I focused on blessing every congregation I visited.

In such an unpredictable activity as booking churches to speak in, I figured out a rule that served me pretty well. If I called a church number and got no answer, I would not leave a message on the answering machine; I preferred to try again at another time of day. If I called a second time and got no answer, I'd leave a message on the answering machine. If I called a third time and got no answer, I would cross the church off my list and assume that a church so cut off from people that it ignored the phone would have little interest in missions.

If I called a church and the pastor himself answered, I would politely go through my prepared calling routine and then ask for a service. If the pastor seemed reluctant, I wouldn't push hard. I assumed that if he or she were answering the phone directly, then the church was small and probably struggling financially. The first rule of church staffing is that the secretary is the first person you hire after you have a pastor. At the same time, if a struggling church wanted me to visit, I would happily take a financial loss in exchange for the opportunity to preach my heart out and bless the church any way I could.

Whenever I got a receptionist on the phone, I knew I had found the Holy Grail. If the church had a receptionist, it likely had a large staff. If it had a large staff, it likely had a vibrant ministry to people and a deep concern for them. If a church had a real concern for people, then I knew they would want to support my vision.

Again, many small churches had a similar concern for people, but large churches were almost a lead-pipe cinch for a good missions offering and a long-term relationship of support.

Having connected to a receptionist, I wouldn't ask to speak to the pastor. I would ask for the pastor's administrative assistant. I saw assistants as the real key to getting off to a good start. Once I got on the phone with the pastor's assistant, I treated them as if they were the pastor. I'd tell them all about myself, my wife, my kids, and ask them about themselves, as well. Then I'd tell about my missionary calling and my hopes of getting a service at the church. Then I'd ask whether the pastor had empowered them to book the schedule, or whether I needed to speak to the pastor. Only in the largest churches were the assistants so empowered, but I never had one feel badly that I had asked. Obviously, such a question amounted to a real vote of confidence in them. Of course, all this time I took notes. At the end of the call, I followed up immediately with a brief thank-you note to remind the assistant of my call.

> **NEVER MISTREAT OR SLIGHT AN ASSISTANT IN ANY WAY. YOU'LL PAY FOR IT IF YOU DO.**

Once I had made friends with the assistants, they would *insist* that their pastor either take my call or call me back. They would tell the pastor what a kind and thoughtful person I was. And then I went to the front of the guest-speaker list, because they had the power to put me there. And best of all, I had made a friend who looked forward to meeting me in person, listening to my sermon, and making sure the decision-makers took up my case quickly in deciding whether to support me.

These same general truths hold true in any area of business. The administrative assistant is a person worth knowing, not only at the basic human level, but also because he or she can become a powerful potential ally for your cause. Never mistreat or slight an assistant in any way. You'll pay for it if you do.

Once you've made friends with the administrative assistant, you'll have a great name to drop.

YOU CAN'T DROP A NAME YOU'VE FORGOTTEN

How can you drop a name you can't remember? I've met leaders with an unbelievable talent for remembering names. I am not one of them.

Anyone in a highly visible position recognizes the phenomenon of having everyone know you while you know hardly any of them. It's the most daunting social reality I face. Often, I become shy in public if everyone there knows who I am and they have a reasonable expectation that I may know them.

I wish I knew the name of every student at Northwest University, but I don't. I confess this fact as a matter of great shame, since my hero in college presidency knows *everyone* at his school. Dr. Robert H. Spence, president of my *alma mater,* Evangel University, served there for nearly forty years and seemed to know the name of everyone who ever set foot on campus. I bow reverently before the master, "just as I am, without one plea . . . " (a little joke for those who remember Billy Graham's wonderful crusades).

If you're like me, you don't know everyone's name, even the names of people you probably should know. If you aren't like me, you won't need any of the following advice, so skip on to the next chapter. But if you struggle to remember names, consider a few guidelines to follow:

- Learn people's names the first time you meet them. In settings of less than ten people, make it a point to learn the names of everyone there. While you may not be able to learn the names of everyone in an organization immediately, you can do it eventually if you split the group into segments. Almost anyone can learn twenty names in a session, if they try. Practice identifying each face in the room, at least a couple of times.

- If you're in charge of events where you'll be meeting new people, make sure name tags are offered at the registration or entry. Then make it a point to look at the name tags of people you interact with. If they aren't wearing one, ask for their name.

- Say the person's name several times. Don't be silly and obvious about it, but make sure you say it a few times to help drill it into your mind.

- Some people invent mnemonics or memory devices to help them remember people's names. A tall, athletic guy named Wilson might be remembered for Wilson Sporting Goods. A regal, good-looking fellow with a kingly bearing named Castleberry (ahem) might be remembered that way. People sometimes have names that fit their professions, like a philosopher named Wise or a craftsman named Smith. Almost anyone's name can be wrestled into a memory device. A towering guy named Jack or a sweet girl named Mary, who reminds you of the mother of Jesus, might be thought of in those ways to connect them with their names. I actually have a few friends whose names quickly offer themselves to humorous associations of the "Ima Hogg" variety, but if you come up with such a device, keep it to yourself. Scrupulously!

- Ask for a business card and/or write down the names after the meeting. Then review your notes over the next few days. At the end of each day when you empty your pockets, take a moment to pray for each person whose business card you received.

- Write a note to people you've met, letting them know it was nice to meet them or thanking them for some service they provided.

- Add the name to your files. It's almost certain that you have a cellular phone, so make sure you keep their name in your phone for easy reference. In the old days (like, in the 1980s), people used to keep their contacts in an archaic thing called a Rolodex, which provided easy access to contacts. People who knew a lot of folks were said to have a big Rolodex. With the advent of the cellular phone, especially the smart phone, no one has an excuse not to have a big "Rolodex." Keep a running list of all or at least some of the people you've met during the week, and then pray for each of them by name at the end of the week and perhaps again at the end of the month.

- Go to Facebook or LinkedIn as soon as possible and send an invitation to your new friends. This will provide you with all kinds of information about them, as well as a continuously updated photograph. If you sync Facebook to your contacts file for your computer and phone, the picture will transfer automatically to your phone as well. LinkedIn will give you the person's whole résumé.

- Review your Facebook friends periodically to remind yourself of names and faces. Sometimes, you'll actually learn the face before you've met the person because of your electronic connection. While you review them, take time to pray for them as well. Facebook is a terrific prayer list.

- Use Google to find out more about new acquaintances. This exercise will further cement their names into your memory and will tell you more about their business.

- Since this chapter is about name-dropping, it may also be worth finding out who is dropping your name. One way to do that is to Google yourself periodically to see what is being said about you out there in cyberspace. If you find that you've been scorched by someone, it may not be a big deal, but there may also be ways for you to limit damage to your reputation. It can feel painful to find that some blogger has criticized you, but it's better to be aware of it than ignorant of it. You might say that Googling yourself can also let you know who is dropping your name, as well as who may be dropkicking it. You can also set up a Google alert that will send you an email every time your name or your business' name gets posted on the Web. Just go to www.google.com/alerts and then follow the easy instructions to set it up. Google alerts won't report comments about you on social media like Facebook, Twitter, and LinkedIn.

People's names are precious to them. In biblical times, parents often gave their children names to represent their hopes for the future. Names often carry sweet memories of the affection of parents and grandparents, especially family nicknames or "pet" names. In today's world, a person's "name" means their reputation. When you act in someone's name, they lend you their authority. Everyone wants a good name.

> **"**
>
> **WHEN YOU LEARN A PERSON'S NAME AND REMEMBER IT, YOU PAY THEM GREAT RESPECT.**
>
> **"**

When you learn a person's name and remember it, you pay them great respect. When you drop their name appropriately in connecting with their friends and speak well of them, respect converts into honor. Never take names lightly.

WORKING THE NET

1. Take time now to remember three administrative assistants who have served you recently with kindness or efficiency. If you can't remember their names, do some research and recover these valuable resources. Then, take time to write a thank-you note to each one. If they've helped you only once, say thanks for that one time. Let them know that you appreciate the role they play in making their boss look good, making guests feel welcome, or providing some other specific service. You might add how much you appreciate your own assistant (or wish you had one) and what a blessing it is for leaders to have great help. Try to mention some specific way you think their work enhances the mission of their business or organization. Then let them know that you are at their service if you can repay their kind attention.

2. Plan to attend an event soon in which you will meet people you don't know. Look for opportunities to practice dropping names, by the rules. Focus on how you can use existing relationships to establish new ones. Remember that you want to set up the new relationships on a less-than/greater-than basis. One way to do that is to look for a way to serve the people you meet. Seeking ways to serve people will make you bolder in meeting them. As my friend Jeff Rogers says, "It's hard to be nervous when your mind is on service."

CHAPTER TEN

THINK

THE WORK NET

Rob Smith grew up in a country that no longer exists. In the 1960s, when African people began casting off the rule of European kings and taking back their ancestral lands, the British territory of Northern Rhodesia became the new African nation of Zambia. The Smith family shifted back to its native South Africa. But turbulent tides move lots of sand, and in 1977, Rob once again sought out a new land. He moved to the United States but never lost his love for the continent of his birth.

Like many immigrants, he soon became an entrepreneur. He not only started profitable businesses, but also a Christian school and a charitable foundation dedicated to rescuing orphans in Africa. But as a businessman, he quickly wearied of the cycle of dependency that charitable works can generate. He began to see business, rather than charity, as the key to lifting Africans out of poverty and misery.

As CEO of Thain Boatworks, Inc., in Everett, Washington, Rob runs a company that builds ferry boats and pleasure cruisers. As he thought hard about how to combine his talent for business with his concern for African peoples, he found a way to put all his passions into the same project. Combining his love for boats with his compassion for Africa, Rob conceived a new entrepreneurial effort, EarthWise Ventures. But Rob knew he couldn't accomplish the big scope of his vision for transforming African economies by himself.

Like all successful entrepreneurs, Rob began to weave a network to put his vision to work. Together with his partners, he has created an exciting variety of strategies to design free-market solutions to build African infrastructure. He built EarthWise Ventures on the conviction that investing for profit in developing countries serves a philanthropic function because of the economic relief these investments create. The keystone effort of his company is the restoration of ferry traffic on Lake Victoria, serving Uganda, Tanzania, and Kenya.

I first met Rob when he came to speak at my Rotary Club, where I served as the club reporter for the day. (If you're not part of such a service organization, you would do well to join one! They are the ultimate networking clubs, and none better than Rotary.) After I heard his presentation, I recognized a future friend. As a former missionary to Ecuador, I had tried to do something similar to his project . . . and failed. Rob's venture restored my faith in venture philanthropy!

Rob came to the United States at the age of nineteen. Although he has lived here far longer than he lived in Southern Africa, his "blood is still South African." But his passion for Africa doesn't mean he can't clearly see its reality.

"If you had asked me in the 1980s about Africa, I would have said it was hopeless," he says. Having lived throughout southern Africa, he recognizes "it's all a mess, even without apartheid, in terms of measurable indicators." Among its many problems, Africa faces the deadly emergence of the AIDS crisis, a problem of unparalleled dimensions that destroys individual lives even as it debilitates national economies.

"In my perspective as a Christian," Rob says, "true religion is taking care of orphans and widows." [125] Because of the high rate of death from AIDS, parents leave countless orphans in Africa. "My heart was moved, as a Christian man, to impact Africa by raising orphans with a worldview that would address the issues Africa is facing."

As he got involved in purely charitable work through his foundation, Rob began to see the need for greater empowerment of Africans to improve their own destinies. "The Africa I grew up in was a dependent Africa," he says. "I grew up on the mission field, and even the missionaries lived a lifestyle of dependence, raising their funds overseas. I wanted to build a nondependent model of development for Africa."

At first, Rob tried setting up orphanages with their own farms to support them, but he found it difficult to develop a for-profit mentality in a nonprofit organization. To address his concerns, he moved beyond the care of orphans to try to develop the community around them. "It occurred to me that the only thing that can produce sustainable development is free market business. I decided to put my money where my mouth is, investing in business in Africa to produce long-term development."

He explains that in Africa, infrastructure is the main economic problem. "As we looked at how we could enter the private sector in Africa, we decided to lead Americans in investing for profit in infrastructure development," he says, referring to this approach as "missional investing." He adds, "There's a different type of accountability when you're reporting to stockholders instead of donors. Stockholders watch their dollars a lot more closely."

In no way does Rob disapprove of charitable work. "I'm not minimizing donations; after all, I'm deeply committed to Pilgrim Africa (the organization through which his charitable foundation now works). People should continue to give to African organizations that focus on crisis. But for economic uplift, we need more social entrepreneurship in Africa."

Rob loves the nascent social entrepreneurship movement in America. He loves the fact that several colleges across the nation, like Northwest University in the Seattle area, have recently started offering master's degrees in social entrepreneurship. "We have lots of great theory, but fewer practitioners," he recognizes. It turns out that practicing economic development is a lot harder than talking about it.

"In America, one of the world's best business climates, 80 percent of start-ups fail. But the risk is worth taking, even in the more difficult African context. There's never been a better time to invest in Africa. It's yearning for economic freedom and the possibility of profit."

EarthWise Ventures exists to fuel economic infrastructure in Africa. "The ferry system had collapsed on Lake Victoria, even though it was a booming business during colonial times. So we decided to put a ferry system back on the lake." Ventures on water always have a romantic allure, but Rob's project has the additional attraction of environmental value, since the new ferries have bio-oil engines.

EarthWise Ventures worked with Columbia University's mechanical engineering and climate department under the leadership of Jeffrey Sachs to refine the engine for the ferries. Since local entrepreneurs can produce the fuel used by the new engines, profits from the ferry go back into the local community, fueling the development cycle as well as the boats. "You must have customers, or you don't have a business," he explains. "We've decided to be the customer by buying locally produced fuel that we lead the farmers to produce." The ferry has become a full-fledged reality, now working to remake the economy around Lake Victoria.

All entrepreneurial projects face obstacles, and the new ferry system is no exception. "Lake Victoria is inland, so how do you get a thirty-five-ton ferry to it? The roads and bridges are too rickety, dating from the colonial days." Rob used a local Seattle architect to design a ferry that locals could assemble from pieces no more than forty feet long. He shipped the pieces to Africa, and workers assembled them at the lake site. The ferry has a plywood structure and hull with a fiberglass covering. The finished boats cost about $2 million each and EarthWise Ventures networked investors to find the money for two boats.

The current enterprise requires about sixty employees. Each additional boat will hire forty workers. "We want to bless the entire community," Smith beams with satisfaction. The company works with independent local ferry operators to feed passengers into the system, branding the entire service as EarthWise in a way analogous to the way regional air services share the branding of the major airlines. Tickets cost $25–40 dollars, competitive with local bus service. But while both modes of transport cost essentially the same amount, the ferry can reduce a two-day, dangerous bus trip to a water passage of about seven hours. The ferry also serves university students, who come from all the countries surrounding the lake.

Each ferry offers 120 economy and 30 first-class seats. The boats sell cold sandwiches and drinks, thus decreasing the fuel and labor costs of preparing hot food onboard. The minimum occupancy required for profitability is 40 percent. At 60 percent it becomes very profitable, and at 80 percent it becomes lucrative. Baggage costs extra, since the ferry cannot operate overloaded.

Because of the lack of infrastructure, much of Africa never had phone service through landlines. But with the invention of the cell phone, African countries could go directly to mobile phones without having to "pass Go." Since almost every African these days has a cell phone, ferry passengers pay for and receive a barcode on their cell phones that serves as their paperless ticket. Local cell-phone time vendors also profit from the venture, since everyone understands they can use cell-phone time as a currency to buy tickets. (You can look at Rob's work by visiting www.earthwiseventures.com and www.pilgrimafrica.)

Rob Smith, a man moved by the Holy Spirit, is acutely aware of the way God has led him into one of the world's most exciting and morally powerful business ventures. As he creates jobs across East Africa, he does it as an ambassador of the kingdom. He visited my Rotary Club to build his network of investors, as he knew he couldn't do the whole project by himself. He depends on the Spirit's help to weave the right people into his network.

Rob's business provides a great example of what we might call "the work net." The enterprise he's building not only includes the investors he finds, but also the whole network of service and product providers in Africa who will supply his company and the customers who will purchase his services.

Without the net, there is no work. Without the work, the net is useless. But when the net and the work come together, everyone who participates wins.

As Rob's project continues into the long future, the mission of God

> **WHEN THE NET AND THE WORK COME TOGETHER, EVERYONE WHO PARTICIPATES WINS.**

will flourish in East Africa, and Christians will carry the gospel from country to country faster than ever before. The reign of God will thrive in Africa through the obedient investment and labor of this boat builder. No doubt a few fishing nets will get tossed from the boats, even as God works the Big Net that brought the boats there in the first place.

THE GODLINESS OF WORK

God's blessing and the mission it entails means that God's first blessing to human beings was work. Work is not a curse, but a great blessing.

Genesis 2:2 describes God as the first worker: "By the seventh day God had finished the work he had been doing; so on the seventh day he rested from all his work." Genesis 2:15 portrays God as the first employer: "The LORD God took the man and put him in the Garden of Eden to work it and take care of it." Clearly, working and giving others jobs can be a godly thing.

Because God created us for a purpose that depends on our work, God announced our mission in the very first blessing. We have a job to do: having and raising children, spreading out over the earth, and making a life for ourselves by gaining mastery over the things God gave us to work with in the world. As each of us does our part in the work net, all of us share in the benefits when goods and products change hands.

> **AS HUMAN BEINGS TAKE DOMINION OVER THE MANY ASPECTS OF WORK IN THE WORLD, THEY ENGAGE IN THE MISSION OF GOD.**

As human beings take dominion over the many aspects of work in the world, they engage in the mission of God. The way God built the world requires just that kind of divine-human cooperation. Psychologist Howard Gardner has theorized that humans have at least eight different kinds of intelligence, and not everyone has the same talents. [126] The fact that differences exist in God-given talents means that people will naturally become specialists in many kinds of work. Not everyone has a talent for farming or mechanical work or mathematics or music, so it's a good thing other people can serve everyone else in those and other specialties.

God created a world that requires humans to cooperate with each other for the maximum possible benefit. In the same way, humans cannot rule over the creation without cooperating with God. God plays the role of King. God's mission is to reign in all the world. In order for that to happen, God needs subjects. While God could have ruled over the animals without creating humans, God has greatly blessed us by creating us to serve as heaven's regents in the world. (A regent rules in the name of someone else.)

Consider a simple example of the kingdom of God at work in God's mission. Since God created human beings with an appetite for food, God wills that people eat. In order for people to eat, we must have farmers—people to grow crops and raise animals for food. We also must have wholesalers—people who distribute the products of agriculture to buyers who use them. That process implies transportation workers (to haul the products to market) and sales people (to reach individual consumers).

In order for the whole food system to work correctly, some sort of regulation or government also must exist. Without a standard system of weights and measures, farmers could take terrible advantage of people who would starve without their products. The system also requires money, since clumsy barter systems cannot adequately deal with the complexity of human needs and behaviors. Money implies some sort of government, as well as bankers.

> **IDEALLY, WHOEVER PLAYS A ROLE IN MEETING HUMAN NEEDS COOPERATES WITH THE EXERCISE OF GOD'S WILL.**

This small example only begins to describe the complexity of human needs and the systems required to meet them. Ideally, whoever plays a role in meeting human needs cooperates with the exercise of God's will—the exact thing God's reign sets out to accomplish. As Jesus taught us to pray in the Lord's Prayer, "Thy kingdom come; thy will be done." These two clauses say the exactly same thing. The coming of God's kingdom fulfills God's will. When we complete the will of God, we cooperate in God's kingly mission.

Of course, not everyone cooperates in the fulfillment of God's will. For example, someone might argue that prostitutes meet people's God-given sexual needs. But such critics fail to see that God is Holy and doesn't accept some versions of "service." In the first blessing of humanity (Genesis 1:28), God intended to create affectionate homes in which children could grow up in love and stability and instruction in godliness. Prostitution obviously contributes nothing to that goal.

In a similar way, a farmer who unjustly gouges his customers in the middle of a famine so that he takes away everything people have and reduces them to slavery doesn't contribute to God's will. [127] The farmer might contribute to fulfilling the people's need to eat, but committing injustice doesn't accord with God's nature or God's will. God didn't have that sort of "dominion" in mind when He commanded humans to rule over the earth.

> **THE KINGDOM GETS EXPRESSED AND THE WILL OF GOD GETS ACCOMPLISHED WHEN PEOPLE DO THE WORK GOD HAS GIVEN THEM IN ACCORDANCE WITH GOD'S HOLY NATURE.**

The fall of humanity means that people will try to find a million ways to do God's work the wrong way. Providing food, music, government, education, health care, transportation, and other needs doesn't fulfill God's kingly will if these things get done in ways inconsistent with God's nature. If merchants sell spoiled, unhealthful food to unsuspecting consumers; if recording executives use music to incite people to sin; if politicians reduce government to tyranny, etc., then they don't reflect God's nature and they don't honor God. Such perversions of human work don't fulfill God's mission, nor do they express God's kingdom. The kingdom gets expressed and the will of God gets accomplished when people do the work God has given them in accordance with God's holy nature. Doing good things God's way goes a long way toward establishing justice in the world.

NETWORKS AND THE HUMAN MISSION

The social nature of the Trinity had an effect on how God created humans. The Lord made us, after all, in the divine image. Just as the Trinity lives in a society of perfect love and communication, so human beings share a social nature. None of us can live life alone. Human fulfillment requires human interaction. Accordingly, the mission of God requires social networking.

I write these words in San Antonio, Texas, at a fine hotel on the River Walk. Today, I got up, ate breakfast, and attended a worship service. Afterward, I went to lunch with some university president colleagues, some old friends and some new. Then I visited Starbucks to have coffee with a friend and talk about an exciting new initiative for planting churches and raising funds to help with it. Afterward, my wife and I went to the mall and bought me some new clothes because I didn't pack enough. Then I returned to the room to watch a bit of television. Later we went out for supper at a great Tex-Mex restaurant with about 200 colleagues. At the end of the day, I sat down to write.

Imagine the networks of people it took to make this day happen. First, I would not have attended the conference without a lifetime of making the friends and associates it took to get me the job I have, which prompted the invitation to the national church executive conference I attended. Lots of people made the conference possible, from those who set up various kinds of services to those who called on old friends and total strangers to get everything in order.

Second, some colleagues provided me breakfast. They want us to do business with their loan fund, either borrowing or depositing money with their agency. They represent hundreds of people who do that very thing, and all of them had a part in feeding me breakfast. So networking bought my breakfast.

The worship service I attended was arranged by someone who called on local friends to preach and sing and serve communion and work the sound board. They also worked with people they didn't know to set up the room and clean it up afterward. I shared communion with my wife and prayed for the man sitting next to me.

Third, I hadn't made plans for lunch, so when a fellow college president at the service asked Kathleen and me to join him and his wife, I said, "Sure!" Since I used to work for him, I felt delighted to spend some time with him. He invited a new president and his wife to join us, and I also invited another new president to join us. We had a delightful lunch, friends old and new, talking shop and sharing ideas. We'll do more together in the future because of the lunch.

Afterward, I went to Starbucks and met, for the third time, a talented networker who's putting together a national church-planting strategy. We discussed how we might work together to construct a new social-entrepreneurship strategy that will result in church plants.

Of course, to accomplish my friend's proposal, we would need to mobilize university professors and students, church planters, business people, donors, and others. We strategized about how to explain the project to various stakeholders. I don't know how far we'll get with the project, but without this kind of initial networking, such projects can't even get considered. Thousands of people will have to cooperate for the project to succeed, but for now, just a few of us know about it.

After coffee, Kathleen and I went shopping. I always buy clothes on sale or at discount stores, since I'm a general cheapskate. But since I had a bit of an emergency and I knew of no nearby discount store, I had to visit an upscale department store in a mall near the River Walk. Looking through the various brands, I bought some clothes on sale—the nicest such items I've ever purchased. Although I paid twice as much as usual, I bought them on sale at half their normal price.

I used my smart phone to research the brand name and found that one of the richest men in the world had recently purchased the company. I found the history of the company quite interesting, as it involved lots of takeovers and mergers and such. It amazed me to think about all the networking that occurred, literally around the world, in order to provide those well-known brand-name items for me. People told their friends to apply for work at the factories. Supervisors did their parts, transportation workers carried the goods across land and sea and maybe air. Workers stocked the shelves, posted the prices, and distributed the sale coupons that sent me into the store in the first place.

People in the mall pointed me to the store. A sales person helped me, and I used a credit card that people at my bank helped to provide. What a vast network of people worked together, just so I could buy some much-needed clothing!

Back at my hotel room, nicely cleaned up by the hotel staff, I watched football. The eighty football players on the field represented only a tiny section of the vast network that put them there. (My office at Northwest University is in a building that we used to rent to a professional football team, so I have a pretty good idea of all the networking that goes into putting a professional football team on the field.) It requires the whole NFL; all teams must exist for one to exist. It requires the folks at the stadium who attend the game, the workers at the stadium, and the television networks. Watching football games involves a lot of unseen networking!

> **IF YOU INTEND TO HAVE ANY LEVEL OF SUCCESS AT ANY LEVEL OF WORK, YOU MUST BUILD A NETWORK OF FRIENDS AND COLLEAGUES TO MAKE IT HAPPEN.**

Finally, I went to supper where an amazing team of workers put on a Tex-Mex feast for 200 people. I spoke Spanish to the Mariachi band and had them play a special song for my wife that I wanted to sing for her (but she pointedly dissuaded me; not all networking works out). But that supper required a lot of relationships, and the sawbuck I slipped the band made me a couple of new temporary friends, too.

At the supper, I sat with a group of church officials who serve as board members of our university. We talked about life, and we talked shop, and we strategized about one thing and another. We prepared some important relational ground for our future.

And now I'm sitting in a chair, in the dark, writing for you by the light of my computer screen. Finally, I am free to write further in this new book! But my day getting to this point literally required the activity of networks all over the country and around the world. That's the way God's mission works. In order for human beings to operate as God's regents in the world, expressing God's kingship and accomplishing God's will, they have to cooperate with God and with each other.

Almost nothing worth doing can be done alone. Even the praying that I will do in just a few moments is more than just me talking to God. First of all, prayer conducted alone leaves out the most important part: the real presence of God. I will pray for friends and for work colleagues. My job—indeed my life and livelihood—depends on hundreds and thousands of people who are a direct part of the things I do, as well as millions of indirect players. As I pray, I try to include as many of them as I can. I ask God to bless my family, friends and co-workers, for God's kingdom to come and for God's will to be done in our lives and in the world.

So, even prayer is an exercise in networking!

If you intend to have any level of success at any level of work, you must build a network of friends and colleagues to make it happen. Whether God has called you to the hardworking, all-day, open-sky life of a farmer, or the mile-a-minute, skyscraper life of a jet-set business executive, the human mission requires an *incredible* web of interactions among people. If it's going to succeed, it also requires fellowship with God.

When we do our network homework—vertically with God and horizontally with people—everyday life can become the fulfillment of the human mission and the expression of the kingdom of God.

WORKING THE NET

In the last section of this chapter, I reflected on the complex web of networking that had made my day possible. Take time to consider all the activities that had to come together to make your day possible.

1. Did anyone provide a service to you during your networking day that deserves a word of thanks? Try to identify at least three people who deserve your gratitude and write them a brief word of thanks, either by email, Facebook message, or a handwritten note. You may want to share with them that you are reading about the mission of God and recognize their service to you as a way they are serving God. Developing a habit of thanking people for their help is a crucial skill in the kingdom net. Be sure to ask whether there is some way you can repay their kindness by serving them.

2. Supply chain is a crucial concept for any success in business. If the supply of goods or services fails, the enterprise fails. If there were any "network failures" that left your activity short of goods or services today, think about how you could strengthen your network to make things run more smoothly. Make a list of people you should connect with to create a more fluid exchange of services. If the network failures were your fault, do you owe a word of apology to anyone?

CHAPTER ELEVEN

DO

WRITING NOTES

A well-written note can make a huge difference in networking. Perhaps one of the most important professional notes I ever wrote followed my interview for the presidency of Northwest University. Visiting the city of Seattle for the first time, I met sixteen members of the Presidential Search Committee in a conference room at the beautiful Hotel 1000 on First Avenue, and we hit it off right from the start. When I finished the interview and returned to my room, I felt the confirmation of God that I would become the next president of Northwest.

The following day, I flew to Fort Worth, Texas. I knew the committee would meet with another finalist on the following Wednesday, and I wanted to send each of them an appropriate follow-up note. I remembered an old dating trick that advises the right course of action: If you know that the girl you went out with Friday is going out with another guy on Saturday, then send her flowers to arrive just before he picks her up for the date. That way, you take up all the space in her head while he's taking your space in her calendar.

Occasionally when I'm in Fort Worth, I make an effort to visit the Amon Carter Museum of American Art. As I strolled through that fabulous place after my visit to Seattle, I looked for paintings that would speak to me. When I saw Charles Russell's masterwork, *Lewis and Clark on the Lower Columbia* (1905), I knew I had found what I was looking for. [128] The beautiful painting depicts a first contact between two great cultures as Lewis and Clark, along with their guide, Sacagawea, hail canoes full of native Pacific Northwesterners on the Columbia River.

Just as I hoped, I found postcards of the painting at the museum store and bought twenty of them. I wrote a thoughtful note to each member of the search committee. Sincerely rhapsodizing about how the Pacific Northwest and its people had impressed me in our meeting, I conveyed my sense of excitement about the potential of serving Northwest University in the future. I had never written a more heartfelt thank-you note.

I mailed them on Saturday to make sure they would arrive in the personal mailboxes of the committee members on Tuesday, before they could interview the next candidate. I wanted to be in that room! When they took the straw vote, they unanimously agreed that I was their candidate. History unfolded from there.

I have no illusion that I got the job as President of Northwest because I sent a few beautiful and thoughtful thank-you cards. It takes a lot more than that to get your dream job! But at times such details can make the difference between success and failure. And if you really want to establish a kingdom connection, you'll go the extra mile.

Standard practice calls for following up on meetings with a thank-you note; make it your regular habit. But there's a big difference between perfunctory notes and thoughtful notes. Thoughtful notes take serious work, and they also take a little more time. You can't always take time to write such notes, but they can produce powerful results, and they're worth the effort on special occasions or at times when a person has had a potent effect on you. Consider a few guidelines for writing both routine and *thoughtful* notes.

> ## "
> ## THOUGHTFUL NOTES TAKE SERIOUS WORK, AND THEY ALSO TAKE A LITTLE MORE TIME.
> ## "

THE ROUTINE NOTE

Send a note anytime someone has done something nice for you. That's just basic, good manners. In networking, a thank-you note is either required or useful if someone has (1) made time in their busy schedule for you to meet them, (2) gone out of their way to visit you at your office or another location, or (3) sent you a gift.

PERSONAL MEETING FOLLOW-UP NOTE

Reflect on the following example of an effective thank-you note for a gift or attention of a personal nature (notice the formulaic elements of the note).

Date: 12/31/2001

Salutation: Dear David,

Initial thanks: Thank you for inviting me and my family to Lisa's birthday party last night.

Naming of the gift: The food was wonderful,

Suggestion of impact: but we were even more blessed by the honor we felt in joining you in celebrating such a significant personal event.

Compliment: You and Lisa have a real gift for drawing people in and making them feel special.

Recognition of kindness: Thanks again for being so kind to invite us.

Invitation: I look forward to meeting with you again soon. Could we get together again for coffee? I (or "My assistant") will be in touch to work out the details.

First-name farewell: Joe

BUSINESS MEETING FOLLOW-UP NOTE

If the occasion for the note is a business contact, the note will differ slightly from the note above. Consider a more business-like example:

Date: 1/4/2011

Salutation: Dear Mr. Hawkins,

Initial thanks: Thank you for taking time out of your busy schedule to meet with me in your office today.

Naming of the gift: It was most helpful for me to hear more about your personal career (business, work, vision, story, etc.) and to explore ways that we might be of mutual help to each other.

Suggestion of impact: After our meeting, I thought of several new ways we may be able to collaborate.

Compliment: Your company is really doing creative (ground-breaking, important, etc.) work, and it would be exciting for us to be a part of it.

Recognition of kindness: Thanks again for being so kind to offer me your attention.

Invitation: I look forward to meeting with you again soon. Could we get together for coffee sometime next week? I (or "My assistant") will be in touch with you (your assistant) soon to work out the details.

Whole-name closing: Joseph Castleberry (Don't assume the person remembers your whole name. Tell them as often as it feels comfortable.)

Following a format like the preceding can take out a lot of the mystery in writing notes, but take care to mix up your vocabulary and make the notes as context specific as possible. By becoming a disciplined note writer, you can become a much more effective networker. Each little act of sincere courtesy that you add to the relationship ties a little knot in the net, making it stronger and more durable.

> **BY BECOMING A DISCIPLINED NOTE WRITER, YOU CAN BECOME A MUCH MORE EFFECTIVE NETWORKER.**

CASUAL FIRST MEETING FOLLOW-UP NOTE

After a first meeting in which you had an opportunity to speak with someone meaningfully and took their business card, a follow-up note can prove useful. It not only helps the person to remember you, it also refreshes your memory of them. While the following note assumes that the person you have met is "senior" to you, the format works equally well for your peers or juniors. Just change the content to suit the relational context:

Date: 1/15/2011

Salutation: Dear Dr. Watson,

Expression of delight: It was such a pleasure to meet you at the Regional Meeting of the National Sherlock Holmes Society this week.

Elaboration: I really enjoyed hearing your presentation and then talking with you personally during the reception.

Compliment: I'll be looking for your future contributions in articles, books, and conference presentations, as you are clearly a rising star in our field.

Offer of future meeting: If your travels take you to Seattle in the months and years ahead, I would be delighted to invite you to coffee or lunch, or to offer you advice about local hotels or restaurants or other services you may need. (According to your sense of how much the relationship advanced in the first meeting, you may want to offer a more specific meeting, such as "I am planning to be in your city on (specific date) and would enjoy meeting you for coffee. If that would be acceptable, please let me know.")

Reiteration: Again, it was a pleasure to meet you and I hope we will be able to talk again and perhaps collaborate in the future.

Closing: Sincerely,

Whole-name farewell: Joseph Castleberry (You *must* use your first and last names with new contacts.)

You may write networking notes on note cards, but increasingly they get sent by email. I am still a little old fashioned and prefer to send and receive paper notes, so you should probably base your decision about whether to use paper on your estimate of how old-fashioned the recipient seems to you. In any case, an actual email note is far superior to an *unwritten* paper note. Whatever you do, *make sure you send the note.*

FACEBOOK NOTE FORMAT

Another option for such notes is the Facebook or LinkedIn note. If you send the note by Facebook, you may want to conflate the note formats for first-time electronic "friending" and follow-up notes to personal meetings, along the following lines:

Date: 1/15/2011

Salutation: Dear Dr. Watson,

Expression of delight: It was such a pleasure to meet you at the Regional Meeting of the National Sherlock Holmes Society this week.

Elaboration: I really enjoyed hearing your presentation and then talking with you personally during the reception.

Compliment: I'll be looking for your future contributions in articles, books, and conference presentations, as you are clearly a rising star in our field.

Offer of future meeting: If your travels take you to Seattle in the months and years ahead, I would be delighted to invite you to coffee or lunch, or to offer you advice about local hotels or restaurants or other services you may need. (According to your sense of how much the relationship advanced in the first meeting, you may want to offer a more specific meeting, such as "I am planning to be in your city on (specific date) and would enjoy meeting you for coffee. If that would be acceptable, please let me know.")

Invitation to association: In the meantime, I hope you will accept my (Facebook/LinkedIn) request.

Whole-name farewell: Joseph Castleberry

THE THOUGHTFUL NOTE

The thoughtful note differs from the more perfunctory follow-up note. You send this note on special occasions—truly meaningful ones. Such occasions might include the so-called rites of passage, such as a wedding, divorce, a funeral, the birth of a child, graduation from high school or college, graduation of one's children, the publishing of a first book or magnum opus, promotion at work, reception of some honor or award, being called to active duty or discharged honorably from the military, diagnosis of a serious disease, or turning a significant age.

Negative events, such as getting sued or indicted, also call for a thoughtful note. An indictment doesn't mean a verdict of guilty, and a conviction doesn't mean a judgment of worthlessness. Jesus made a special point of recognizing the righteousness of those who visit prisoners (see Matthew 25:39–40). Writing to a friend in prison can make a huge difference in their lives. Writing to people who are being sued or prosecuted may offer them the encouragement they need to keep it all together.

Life passages have extreme importance, as people become far more open to input and influence at such times. *Never* take advantage of people at such moments. The only valid Christian posture is to add benefit to them, and the greatest benefit conceivable is that people should either meet the Lord or grow in their faith. Toward that end, the kingdom networker employs the thoughtful note.

While the thoughtful note doesn't replace a personal phone call or visit, neither does the personal visit replace the note. Notes have an amazing durability, as the recipients can read them over and over again, with potent effect, for many years. Just this week, I paid a surprise visit to a friend in a city far from Seattle and saw a thank-you note I had written several years ago pinned to his note board. He didn't know I would visit, so it must have hung there for years, reminding him of my high estimation of his service to me.

In writing a thoughtful note, don't fail to pray that God would give you "a word" for the recipient. In the best cases, thoughtful notes pronounce a powerful, spiritually effective blessing on the person. They may also constitute a form of prophetic advice, containing what the Bible might call a "word of wisdom" or a "word of knowledge" or

> **THOUGHTFUL NOTES PRONOUNCE A POWERFUL, SPIRITUALLY EFFECTIVE BLESSING ON THE PERSON.**

some other gift of the Holy Spirit. [129] God really can speak to someone through your note!

If you come from a church background that doesn't address such issues, you should think carefully about them. On the other hand, if you come from a Charismatic or Pentecostal background, I plead with you not to overstate your case. You don't need to say you're offering a prophecy or word of wisdom. As Forrest Gump said, "Stupid is as stupid does"; things are recognized by their fruit. [130] It's equally true that "wisdom is as wisdom does" (and prophecy is as prophecy does). If you succeed at delivering a word from God to someone, you won't have to tell them that you did it. They will recognize it soon enough. Definitely don't dress up your words in some sort of King-James-hyper-religious language. To the great majority of people, you will look ridiculous.

It may seem simplistic to suggest that the thoughtful note could have a format, since by definition, such notes burst with thought and creativity. Nevertheless, a format can help you to channel your thoughts. For example:

Date: December 30, 2010
Greeting: Dear Mary,
Introduction: Although we spoke briefly a few days ago, I am writing to express more deeply my sorrow over Bill's death.

Prayer (and it better be true): I had been praying for him fervently for the last several years, holding on to real hopes that the Lord might grant him a whole new season of life and ministry.

Offer of theological insight: As I wrote on my Facebook page the following day, Bill never surrendered to cancer, but rather, to the sovereign will of the Lord who decided, once and for all, to heal him.

Expression of appreciation: We've all been inspired for years at the way he responded to the contradiction of illness, and now we are inspired by his faithfulness to the end. Although I didn't get to spend a lot of time with Bill, I learned a lot from him.

Example: I've been using him as an example in the doctoral classes I teach. His teachings on faith were wonderfully illustrated by the heroic life of faith that he lived.

Offer of prayer: As the New Year dawns and you get through the hard weeks before and after the memorial service, I will keep you in prayer, as always, and I look forward to great things in your life as the Lord's goodness reveals itself in brand new ways.

Thoughtful reflection: Life in the mortal body is certainly full of contradictions, but none of them sully the absolute truth that God's goodness and mercy endure forever.

Prophecy of blessing: In the days ahead, you will rise up, shaken but not shattered, and you will begin again to live out actively and publicly the deep character that God has been working into you for so many years. I have fond hopes that my family and I will be honored of God to have a part in the next chapter of your life. We have exciting work to do together, and many satisfactions ahead.

Offer of service: Please know that I am at your service. I'd be delighted to receive a phone call from you at any time. My mobile phone number is 000-000-0000.

Closing: Blessings,

Name: Joseph Castleberry

Such a note may seem like a fine sympathy note for someone who has lost a loved one, but how might the same format look for someone who has experienced the birth of a new child or grandchild?

Let's assume that the new parents have no commitment to Christ. Nobody, even atheists like the late Christopher Hitchens, gets upset that people have sincerely prayed for them, and everyone loves having a blessing pronounced on them. Here is what a similar note might look like:

Date: December 25, 2010

Greeting: Dear Robert and Julie,

Introduction: Congratulations on the birth of your first child!

Prayer (and it better be true): I've been praying for you and your baby regularly over the past few months, and I'm so delighted to see your prayers and mine answered in the arrival of this marvelous, healthy child.

Offer of theological insight: The Bible assures us that God has a special plan for the life of your child, and it will be exciting to see how God works it out in the years ahead.

Expression of appreciation: The birth of a new generation of your family really promises to be a blessing to the world. Your family's tradition of love and good works will live on through this baby. (Whatever you say here, make sure it's based on truths you have discussed with the parents. You might just say something like, "with such fine parents, this baby has a wonderful future.")

Example: I can't help thinking of the time when you helped Kathleen and me move into our new home. We were so sore at the end of the day, and you worked as hard as we did. It's heartwarming to think that you'll be passing on the same values of friendship to your child.

Offer of prayer: I have added your baby's name to my prayer list, and I will think of you often as you raise this special child.

Thoughtful reflection: Child-raising has been the most challenging thing I've ever faced, but nothing has ever been more rewarding.

Prophecy of blessing: As your baby grows, I pray that he will be a quick and lifelong learner. I pray that God might protect him from serious illness and deliver him from tragedy. As he goes to school, may he excel in his own special talents, be well-accompanied by faithful friends, and be loved by people who will sacrifice to help him succeed. I pray that he will gain an early sense of purpose in life and never be bored or not know what to do. May he find his ideal helper at the right time, and may he provide your family with a new generation to carry out your values and traditions. May he live a long and fruitful life and know God's favor throughout every situation.

Offer of service: Please know that Kathleen and I are always ready to help you in any way we can. You can consider this note as a coupon for a free baby-sitting session as soon as you are ready to leave the child for a few hours. My direct number is 000-000-0000.

Closing: Blessings,

Name: Joe

Obviously, you can't just copy this note. Do some thinking to figure out what you want to say in each step of the format, as well as smoothing it all together so that it reads fluidly. We call it a "thoughtful note" because of the thinking you do to create it.

Whether it celebrates the arrival of a baby or a book or an award, or whether it marks the occasion of tragedy or triumph or trouble, a thoughtful note is the networking equivalent of heavy artillery. It can make a real impact and clears the ground for the forceful advance of the kingdom.

> **THOUGHTFUL NOTES GET PLACED IN SCRAPBOOKS, KEPT IN BIBLES, OR OTHERWISE PRESERVED FOR POSTERITY.**

In most cases, perfunctory notes get acknowledged and promptly tossed in the "circular file-basket." Thoughtful notes, on the other hand, get placed in scrapbooks, kept in Bibles, or otherwise preserved for posterity. I've heard from people about how they framed my baby-prophecy notes (similar to the totally fictitious example above) and hung them in the child's room. Such notes will really bless the folks who receive them. God will work through them to either expand or strengthen the kingdom net, and you will be remembered forever for "a word fitly written in due season."

WORKING THE NET

Becoming an accomplished note writer takes practice. Take the time now to begin.

1. Write a *Personal Meeting Follow-Up Note,* following the format suggested earlier. You can use paper or send an email or social media note, depending on your preference. If you haven't had a personal meeting to follow-up on, arrange for that now and write the note afterward. It's time to start networking!

2. Write a *Business Meeting Follow-Up Note.* Be sure to actually send the note.

3. Write a *Casual First-Time Meeting Follow-Up Note* based on a real meeting.

4. Using the format for the *Thoughtful Note,* write a note to someone you know who has just experienced a major life event. Go back and re-read that section and give it a try. Again, be sure to actually send the note. Don't be shy, since your thoughts are going to bless someone.

CHAPTER TWELVE

THINK

WHAT IS THE CHURCH?

What is the church, and what is its role in the kingdom net? The church is the vast network of believers united in following Jesus and carrying out the mission of God in the world. The church provides the visible proof of the kingdom net—the whole community of individuals caught up in God's mission. In God's kingdom net, we find both good fish and bad, and Jesus will sort out who's who in the end. But the true church is made up of those who will be left in, after the bad fish have been "culled out." The true church consists of those who have been called out of the sin-stained system of the world and placed into the kingdom of God. Everyone who is in this kingdom is also in the church. Some bad fish found in churches have been caught up in the kingdom net, but they have no place in the kingdom. As Jesus' parable suggests, the angels will sort them out later.

No one can separate the kingdom net and the church. To make the most of the kingdom net and of our networking for God, we must take the church seriously and make a place for it in our lives and our personal practice of faith. Anyone who belongs to the kingdom net must find their place in the church.

The Nicene Creed, a statement of Christian faith that dates back to AD 325, gives us a great description of the true church. It refers to the church as "one, holy, catholic, and apostolic church." For centuries, theologians have referred to these elements as the "Four Marks of the Church." As kingdom networkers, we must understand these marks of the church. [131]

THE ONENESS OF THE CHURCH

The true church can never be *sectarian*. Sectarian churches see their members as the only true Christians. No matter how many congregations or communities may arise to claim the exclusive favor of God, none will ever have it. The one true church includes all those who confess Jesus as Lord and who seek to obey His commands.

Theologians have long called this sense of the church "the invisible church" because no one but God can ever see it all at once. In contrast to the invisible church, we have no choice but to attend visible churches—particular local congregations (and the associations to which they belong, if any). No, you don't have the choice to go it alone. The kingdom net allows for no "virtual private networks."

Although the visible church takes many forms, the invisible church doesn't consist in any particular group of Christians who have made a hard separation between themselves and the rest of the kingdom net because of their doctrinal particularities. We can more accurately describe such groups as sects, a Latin-derived word for "cuts." They have cut themselves off from the kingdom net and proclaimed themselves to be the whole net. Their membership in the body of Christ is in question, not because the body has rejected them, but because they have rejected the body. Like the people to whom Paul wrote in 1 Corinthians 11, their misguided services of Holy Communion bring them under judgment because they don't recognize the body of Christ. [132] May Jesus have mercy on them!

I often say that I recognize the Christian faith of everyone who recognizes mine. If people recognize me as a Christian and confess faith in the same Jesus I believe in, I tend to give them the benefit of the doubt. Jesus' parable tells us that "bad fish" get caught up in the kingdom net, and I've met some pretty stinky ones. (Have you ever actually smelled a used fishnet? No wonder the church can seem a bit stinky at times!) I know some Christians have held their nose around me, too. But it's not our place to sniff at each other too much.

While I just wrote theoretically about the dangers of sectarianism, I'm pretty careful about not throwing that accusation at specific individuals. If I don't like the way some people practice Christianity, then I need to pray for them and engage them in constructive dialogue, not "categorize" them. The Greek word for *accuse*—that thing Satan does to our brothers and sisters in Christ—is *katagoreo*. In some ways, to categorize people is to

> **IF PEOPLE RECOGNIZE ME AS A CHRISTIAN AND CONFESS FAITH IN THE SAME JESUS I BELIEVE IN, I TEND TO GIVE THEM THE BENEFIT OF THE DOUBT.**

> **WE SHOULD ACT GRACIOUSLY TOWARD ONE ANOTHER WHILE AT THE SAME TIME GOADING EACH OTHER ON TO HOLIER LIVES.**

accuse them. We need to be circumspect about accusing people by categorizing them. [133] The angels will sort us out later.

A recent statistic published in *Christianity Today* revealed an amazing fact. Some 48 percent of evangelical Christians "listed violence, hatred, bigotry, intolerance, and lack of love for others" as "negative contributions of the Christian population to American society." In contrast, only 25 percent of the American population in general accused Christians of such things. [134] (Keep in mind, the whole population number is inflated by the 40 percent of us who call ourselves Evangelicals.) Clearly, we feel a lot more sensitive to our smelliness than do our fellow citizens. This harsh judgment of each other as Christians probably stems from the guilt we feel over "falling short of the glory of God." It may also come from a certain self-righteousness that attaches itself, like a leach, to overly religious folks.

We should act graciously toward one another while at the same time goading each other on to holier lives. Still, if people prove themselves unreliable as followers of Jesus, we may choose to avoid them as much as we can. As for me, I have decided to treat all claimants to faith in Christ with grace and to pray that we will all come to unity and maturity in the faith as Christ leads us. [135] Jean-Paul Sartre once said in a play, "Hell is other people." [136] He seemed to have at least a fraction of a point; but hell is *not* other Christians, or other people in general. The church is one, and to paraphrase an old song, "when the saints go marching in, we want to be in that number."

THE CHURCH IS HOLY

Speaking of saints, the word *saint* means "set apart, holy." And so the church is also confessed to be holy. It is so for no other reason than this: Jesus has made it holy by His death on the cross and by the pronouncement of His word. Ephesians 5:25–27 says:

> Husbands, love your wives, as Christ loved the church and gave himself up for her, to make her holy, cleansing her by the washing with water through the word, and to present her to himself as a radiant church, without stain or wrinkle or any other blemish, but holy and blameless.

The church isn't holy because its members live in perfect holiness, but rather because of what Jesus has done. Hebrews 10:14 says, "By one sacrifice he has made perfect forever those who are being made holy." God has declared us perfect, and Christ is not ashamed of us. He makes us progressively holier, and He will present us one day as His glorious bride without spot or wrinkle. As we march toward that day, Christ has set a standard He expects the members of the church to try to live up to.

I grew up around churches strongly influenced by "the holiness movement."

CHRIST HAS SET A STANDARD HE EXPECTS THE MEMBERS OF THE CHURCH TO TRY TO LIVE UP TO.

> **SIN RIPS UP THE NET TOO MUCH. TO KEEP CATCHING FISH, WE MUST KEEP THE NET INTACT.**

Holiness churches believe Christians can live holy lives, and my family owes a lot to the holiness churches. My mother grew up in the Church of the Nazarene, a great example of a holiness church. On my father's side, my great, great-grandmother Nancy Little was led to Christ by a "holiness lady" in the neighborhood, and my great-grandfather Jody joined the holiness movement at a crucial point in his spiritual life, as well.

After my father's family joined the denomination to which I still belong, we had many discussions in our family about the nature of the Christian's sanctification (God's act of making us holy). My great-grandfather Jody always believed he had been entirely sanctified in a moment. My grandfather Joseph believed that sanctification was progressive, but by the time he got to the age when his father had been "entirely sanctified," he believed he had finally achieved entire sanctification. It would appear that some sins, perhaps even *most* sins you can actively commit and not just imagine in your heart, get easier to avoid as we age.

I don't know whether Christians can really live a life of sinless perfection, but I know I can't do it as yet. I still do and say and think things I later regret that call for repentance. I know that I'm growing in Christ as I get older, and as I always say, "maturity looks good on all of us." Growth in holiness does seem consistently tied to the life cycle. Still, experience has taught me to be skeptical of anyone's claim to sinless perfection, regardless of age.

In today's churches, I hear little preaching about holiness—a serious error, I believe. Individual Christians and the many groups to which they belong as believers must never stop striving to live the holiest lives possible, rejecting sin and the indulgence of sinful habits. We all sometimes fail, but the holiness of the church means that we can never yield ourselves to a lifestyle of sin. Sin rips up the net too much. To keep catching fish, we must keep the net intact.

THE CHURCH IS CATHOLIC

What does it mean that the true church is catholic? The last several popes have definitely been men worthy of deep respect. But catholicity doesn't imply that the church is subject to the bishop of Rome. As my friend, the eminent theologian Veli-Matti Kärkkäinen, once pointed out to me, the word *catholic* is an English rendering of the Greek words *kath holon,* or "according to the whole." That phrase has a geographical sense inasmuch as it refers to the whole world. The catholicity of the church insists on the worldwide extension of the church to all nations.

I believe that the true church always remains concerned about the spread of the gospel to all people. The catholicity of the church drives local churches to enter into networks with other local churches around the world. A local church with no direct link to local churches in other countries risks becoming "un-catholic," and thus lacking a mark of God's true church.

But as Dr. Kärkkäinen pointed out to me, there's more to being catholic than just the geographical dimension. A church's preaching has to be *kath holon* as well. In other words, churches must preach the gospel "according to the whole." Back in the early twentieth century, some churches in America began to refer to themselves as "full gospel" churches. Such churches felt impressed by the revival movements of the nineteenth century that had restored certain emphases to Christian doctrine that they believed had gone missing for centuries.

Among the doctrines of the full gospel was the sanctification of the believer; the literal and physical second coming of Christ; and an empowering encounter with the Holy Spirit. They expressed horror at the denial of the miracles recorded in the Bible by the emerging liberal churches, and stood firm on basic Christian truths such as the virgin birth, the sinless life of Christ, His miracles, His atoning sacrificial death, and the bodily resurrection of Jesus.

Preaching the catholic gospel—the gospel-according-to-the-whole—means preaching *all* of the good news about the kingdom. Jesus saves, heals, and empowers by the Spirit. He will indeed return to rule in the kingdom. But He also calls on us to demonstrate the values of the kingdom, providing glimpses into it as we re-engage the human mission. The full gospel means full bellies for the hungry, full access to opportunity for the oppressed, full freedom to pursue our callings and dreams, full lives in every sense. God's kingdom declares good news to the poor, the mourners, the persecuted, the rejected, and the despised. It promises them the eventual overthrow of evil's *régime,* the immediate presence of God to rule in their own lives, and at least partial exterior evidence of the kingdom coming now. It promises to weave members of

> **THE TRUE CHURCH PREACHES THE WHOLE MESSAGE OF THE KINGDOM.**

the whole human family together into the kingdom net. The true church preaches the whole message of the kingdom.

THE CHURCH IS APOSTOLIC

The apostolicity of the church is a mark every bit as crucial as the others. Roman Catholic tradition seeks to guarantee the apostolicity of the church through what it calls "apostolic succession." At the simplest level, apostolic succession means that the apostles anointed successors, who anointed their own successors, who anointed successors, and so on. The chain continues unbroken through the centuries to the present day. Apostolic succession also means that the church continues faithfully in the teaching of the original twelve apostles.

While I don't endorse the Roman Catholic idea of apostolic succession, I'm satisfied that ministers today around the world do indeed stand in apostolic succession. In fact, some self-anointed leaders have successfully founded and led churches without claiming a "daisy-chain" relationship of ordination from the earliest apostles. But surely, that's not what really matters. Ordination is not a magical, shamanistic practice. That is, the anointing doesn't magically flow out of the hands of the anointer and into the anointed one. All true anointing for ministry comes directly from the Holy Spirit, and all rational knowledge of the gospel comes from the Bible and the apostolic tradition of the church. If preachers declare the apostolic message about Christ in the power of the Spirit, no one can legitimately argue that the message lacks "apostolic succession." It really doesn't matter who has laid their hands on the preachers if *God's* hand is on them!

For me, what makes a church apostolic is the same thing that made the apostles apostolic. The word *apostle* is related to the Greek word *apostello,* which means "I send." Jesus directly sent the original apostles into mission. After them, Jesus kept on sending people into the mission of the church, and they became "apostles," too. The New Testament refers to several individuals as apostles who were not original disciples of Jesus (the apostle Paul not the least of them). While this is not the place for a detailed discussion about what an apostle is, I'll just say that Jesus has never quit sending people into mission. In that sense, there have always been apostles in the church.

So, the church is truly the church when the ones who have been "called out" are sent back in! The local church assembled on Sunday doesn't tell the most interesting part of the story. The church is at its best and most interesting when it goes out into the world to accomplish the mission of God. As Emil Brunner once said, "The Church exists by mission as a flame exists by burning." [137] To be the church, we must be both called out and then apostolically sent back in.

This apostolicity includes those sent out as missionaries. But *all* of God's people who embrace the mission of humanity are apostolic. They all express the kingdom of God through their obedience to the full range of callings the Spirit distributes among God's servants:

> Doctors, lawyers, engineers, chiefs;
> business folk, farmers, soldiers, police;
> undertakers, chefs and bakers, toll-takers, scientists;
> school teachers, street preachers, innkeepers, priests.

Excuse me for breaking into a little rap, but I got excited. All of these people, and more, represent the church in the field of God's mission as they walk out their obedience to the rule of God. They fulfill the human mission while carrying out the mission of the church, using their personal, professional, and social networks as conduits for the kingdom to spread.

A great example is the work of Jeff Rogers, a friend of mine from the Seattle area. Jeff is one of the most impressive networkers I've ever met in the kingdom. He not only seems to know everyone in the Seattle area, but he has an amazing gift for making all of us think of him as a close friend. Jeff has an incredible capacity for friendship. No wonder that in his business career, he has established a reputation as a super salesman! He has an uncanny ability to recruit, train, and deploy other sales professionals.

Jeff is the consummate networker in his for-profit businesses. But his passion for the kingdom of God has also driven him to build an amazing network of Christian business people in the cities of Seattle and Bellevue. One of his nonprofit organizations, Kiros, has gathered thousands of area Christians in monthly breakfast meetings designed to connect business people to each other and train them for the expression of God's kingdom in the world of business. His Kiros Transitions ministry has helped hundreds of people find new career connections.

> **"THE CHURCH IS AT ITS BEST AND MOST INTERESTING WHEN IT GOES OUT INTO THE WORLD TO ACCOMPLISH THE MISSION OF GOD."**

Jeff also helped to found another ministry called Linking Shields. That group focuses on serving churches and the clergy in our community. For a time, it also sponsored (and paid for) a monthly luncheon for pastors that facilitated unity, friendship, and prayer. Many interchurch relationships arose from those wonderful lunches. Linking Shields has also gathered thousands of Christian men together to hear top Christian speakers and gain inspiration for living out their faith while engaged in the community.

If that weren't enough, Jeff has established relationships in a number of foreign countries. After his family became particularly touched by the needs of Uganda, they established a foundation, Doingood, that partners with organizations to develop prospective businesses in Uganda. The ministry trains people in solid business principles and empowers them to take on the economic development of their country. Using his American networks, Jeff recruits top business people to travel to Uganda at their own expense to teach business to locals. In the process, they take home lessons from the Ugandans that turn their investment in others into a valuable personal benefit.

Jeff's business life—and the business of the people who work with him—glorifies God and declares the love of God in Christ, in his own backyard or in far-flung places around the globe. No bishop has ever laid hands on him to ensure his apostolic succession and declare him a clergyman. But the fact that Jesus has laid hands on him makes his work apostolic.

So the church is apostolic, not just because of some transgenerational "laying on of hands" by bishops and their successors. In fact, Jesus has *never* taken His hand off of the church! Throughout almost 2,000 years of history, Jesus has never stopped sending the church into mission. He keeps anointing us by the Holy Spirit. He keeps enlarging the kingdom net through our evangelizing work and relationships. He keeps expanding the church to every nation, people, tongue, and tribe through our missionary work. He keeps showing glimpses of the kingdom in society through the work of our hands and the creations of our imagination. All of this continuance maintains the apostolicity of the church.

What I said earlier bears repeating now: A local church with no direct link to local churches in other countries is in danger of being "un-catholic." Just as seriously, it runs the risk of being "un-apostolic." It usually doesn't get the oneness thing, either. And I suspect you won't find it particularly holy. No matter where in the world it may be, show me a church with no intercultural mission effort, and I'll show you either an immature church or a deformed one.

I've seen poor people all over the world enjoy the dignity of contributing to foreign missions. They support their missionaries, sometimes in prayer alone, but almost always with sacrificial financial giving as well. People can have no bigger blessing than to be involved in the biggest thing in the world.

> **THERE IS NO CHURCH TOO SMALL, TOO POOR, OR TOO HUMBLE TO PARTICIPATE FULLY IN THE KINGDOM.**

C. S. Lewis once said that at Bethlehem, something bigger than the world itself fit into a small manger. [138] Like Jesus, the kingdom is bigger than the world itself—but there is no church too small, too poor, or too humble to participate fully in the kingdom.

CHRISTIANS, CHURCHES, AND KINGDOM NETWORKING

The priority of God's global mission inevitably leads individual congregations to seek out partners. The mission is too large and the workers too few for any one congregation to go it alone. So local congregations committed to the *missio ecclesiae* both seed and seek out partner congregations.

I remember when my local congregation at the time, Nassau Christian Center in Princeton, New Jersey, sent out eighteen active missionaries. Several went to foreign countries, and others became church planters in America. Our little congregation had no way to adequately support them all. In many denominations, member churches usually network with each other to support each other's missionaries. They cooperate on other issues related to their mission by credentialing ministers, training ministers in Bible colleges or seminaries, publishing discipleship materials, and other projects, all of it good.

I've spent most of my pastoral and missionary career as a denominational insider. By that, I mean that I conceived of Christian life almost entirely as something to be lived inside my denomination. I didn't often seek out relationships with Christians of other denominations. I had all the Christian fellowship and work relationships and even financial support I felt I could manage inside my own group. Such an exclusive posture has become increasingly rare in today's church. As a mega-church pastor friend of mine once said, "I reserve the right to get smarter."

So I no longer see such isolation as favorable. Still, some wonderful advantages can be had through cooperation with fellow believers who all start pretty much from the same place and with the same expectations.

As a denominational minister, I felt that I had a real advantage over independent ministers. In my view, independents didn't have enough authority over them. Who would help them if they wandered into mistakes, heresies, or moral failures? But the main reason I didn't envy the free air of independence involved relationships. It seemed to me that independent ministers didn't have the network of relationships that I enjoyed in my denomination. Our denomination has churches in more than 200 countries and political units around the world. It has always amazed me how easy it seems to make friends immediately within our denomination. We can quickly plan great projects with people from every nation on earth.

A few years ago, I became a seminary dean and then a college president. I started seeing the critical importance of building friendships from a broader range of churches. Colleges usually cannot work at the same level of denominational isolation as local churches often do. I know that Northwest University cannot and should not work that way. As I befriended more independent ministers, I came to a shocking conclusion: They networked even more intentionally than I did! As a matter of fact, I know many independent pastors who put me to shame as a networker. Their work in building friendships with ministers all over the world helped me understand that *all* kingdom work requires an active approach to networking.

Inside the warm fellowship of a denomination, we find it easy to take a passive approach to building networks. Our elected leaders carry the responsibility for holding the fellowship together. They plan regional and local meetings. They manage health insurance and retirement plans. They coordinate missionary efforts and promote denominationally sponsored colleges and carry out other denominational tasks.

Missionaries in denominations often network brilliantly, especially in those groups that believe in "faith missions." Building a group of about 100 or more churches to support their work, they carefully stay in touch with that financial lifeline from whatever far-flung locale they may minister.

> **BEING PART OF A DENOMINATION BRINGS AWESOME BENEFITS, BUT IT SHOULDN'T BECOME A TRAP THAT LEADS TO PASSIVITY IN NETWORKING.**

But often, a denominational pastor has the luxury of having the network brought to him or her. They seem to have no need to get overly intentional about networking. Independent pastors, on the other hand, *have* to get much more aggressive in their networking. If they don't go out and make a network, they won't have one. An intentional and aggressive commitment to thick networking—inside the church and outside—may in fact be one of the main reasons that independent churches are growing faster than denominational churches in America. [139] Being part of a denomination brings awesome benefits, but it shouldn't become a trap that leads to passivity in networking.

One might think that the essence of pastoral work is networking. I think that a certain kind of networking is indeed the essence of effective pastoral work. But most church leaders don't seem as vigorous in their networking as they might be. The median size for churches in the United States is around 75 members. [140] From that fact, it would seem that most pastors manage to carry out their ministry in a fairly small social circle—say, some 500 to 1,000 people.

Such a small circle can result in a warm community of believers, but those communities can often become too inwardly focused. Without a vigorous process of continual, conscious networking, the circle doesn't grow. And a stagnant church has a hard time explaining how it is following Jesus and obeying the Great Commission. I mean no condemnation here, as reasons may exist as to why a particular church cannot grow in its specific location. But such churches will always feel that something important is missing. If a church really cannot grow because of its location, then it has an extra heavy responsibility to help churches grow in other places. That requires them to get deeply involved in the Great Commission by sending, giving, and praying.

WORKING THE NET

1. Does your church cooperate with other Christians in the task of world missions? Does it support world evangelization financially on a regular basis? If not, you may miss out on the blessings of participating in world missions. Don't just give independently. Go to your pastor or session or other leadership structure and let them know that you want the church to give to missions on a monthly basis and that you will make the first pledge. Ask the church to agree that your offering will be sent to a ministry that you can agree on together. Urge your pastor to invite a missionary to speak at your church and to give other members an opportunity to give to missions through the church. Work to build a network of missionary outreach in different parts of the world through your local church.

2. Begin to regularly read a mission magazine or website to learn about missions. Learn about unreached people groups, frontier missions, Christian relief and development, opportunities to serve, etc. You would do best to start with your church's denominational mission board, which you can find easily on any Internet search engine. A few examples include:

   - Mission Frontiers (http://www.missionfrontiers.org)
   - Assemblies of God World Missions (http://worldmissions.ag.org)
   - International Missions Board of the Southern Baptist Convention (http://www.imb.org/main/default.asp)
   - World Vision (http://www.worldvision.org/)
   - Frontiers (http://frontiers.org)

3. Take a short-term missions trip and experience the international church. Even if your local church can't organize such a trip, many mission agencies coordinate them and will accept you as a team member. Virtually every denomination has such an agency, and you can find out more from local or national offices of your denomination, which are easy to find online. If you attend an independent church, YWAM may be a good option for you (http://www.ywam.org). Just go to the website and you'll see opportunities all over the world. A host of other short-term opportunities can be found at http://www.shorttermmissions. com/org/.

4. Whether you're scheduling your first short-term mission experience or your twentieth, remember that you're not just looking for an experience, but rather for kingdom connections that you can use for your own ministry and network. That may or may not mean establishing direct, enduring relationships with people in another country. Ideally it means connecting with mission agencies that can continue connecting you and your network to the worldwide church.

5. If you do make friends in a foreign country, I urge you *not* to let your relationship become a direct financial one. The point of world missions is not to become a private channel of funding from one country to another. There are a million ways for private finance of international workers to go wrong, and *relationships that become based on money always go sour.* Save yourself the heartache. The best way to avoid making grave mistakes is to give financial support through established mission agencies.

Always consult with the mission partner who took you to a place before giving money. Missionaries are not infallible, but they know more about foreign missions than amateurs do and a wise kingdom networker works the whole net, not just a single node. Let the network work.

CHAPTER THIRTEEN

THINK

THE CHURCH AND CHANGE

T he church is God's greatest instrument for expanding the kingdom net. Vast in its reach, the church constantly moves. As Jesus said of the kingdom, so today's church advances forcefully, and violent people take it by force. [141] Four times more Christians live in the world today than a hundred years ago. [142] In the midst of so much change and movement, anyone who would attack the church will find it a moving target. Whoever wishes to criticize the church will have to answer the question, "Which church?"

No one sees the church changing more clearly than those who study church history. To grasp the state of Christianity in America today, it helps to take a tour through history. The story of my own family's religious experience over some 300 years in America has taught me a lot about where we currently stand. It suggests how churches change in fascinating ways over time—and it is a network story. It illustrates how networking has shaped the church in our history and shows why today's churches have the opportunity to become more networked than ever.

HEINRICH KESSELBERG MOVES TO AMERICA

Back in 1683, Heinrich Kesselberg came to America from Germany as part of the first group of Mennonites who joined William Penn's colony in Philadelphia. The Mennonites were and are beautiful people, committed to radical Christian discipleship and peacemaking. Henry had worked in a paper mill in Germany and apparently came to America to scout out the situation for William Rittenhouse. Later, they would build America's first paper mill in Pennsylvania. When Heinrich bought property in 1691, a new American surname grew out of his old German one. He became Henry Castleberry.

> **PIONEER FAMILIES FOUND IT ALMOST IMPOSSIBLE TO SURVIVE UNLESS THEY HAD A SOLID CLAN OF PEOPLE AROUND THEM TO OFFER ASSISTANCE, SECURITY, AND FRIENDSHIPS.**

From the sketchy history that remains, it appears that Henry wasn't a very good Mennonite, but he does seem to have been a good networker. Whatever the case, none of his children chose to remain Mennonites. Rather than speaking German in a tight community outside Philadelphia, they spread out. They entered a larger world and adopted English as their first language. Most of them became Anglicans and joined Episcopal churches.

One of Henry's sons, William, went his own way. Marrying a Welsh girl named Margaret Davis, William moved to Bucks County and joined the New Britain Baptist Church. As he left the German Mennonites and joined with the English-speaking Baptists, he found that his new network of friends would not accept his old baptism. The problem? He'd been sprinkled, not completely dunked under water. So, William got baptized again. [143]

Perhaps William felt completely convinced by the biblical arguments of his new Baptist friends. Or perhaps he needed his new friends too much to hold onto the standards of his previous neighbors. Regardless of his true convictions, he literally took the plunge so he could enter a new expression of the body of Christ.

Apparently, William's second baptism "took." Within a few years, he and Margaret moved down to Harrisonburg, Virginia, where they became charter members of the Linfield Creek Baptist Church. They founded the church along with Samuel Newman, an early Baptist preacher, and his family. Their relationship with the Newmans and other early Baptist families resulted in a firm alliance that created a stable community of pioneers. Over several generations, they migrated down the east coast, and together, they and their children and grandchildren planted several of the earliest Baptist churches in America—a great strategy for populating and civilizing the wild American frontier.

FRONTIER RELIGION

Frontier life could be exceedingly dangerous. Lone settlers or pioneer families found it almost impossible to survive unless they had a solid clan of people around them to offer assistance, security, and friendships. In America's history, perhaps churches played the most important unifying role for such clans. Church membership often served as the most important marker of who was in the group and who was not. Doctrine played an extremely important part in maintaining the boundaries of the clan.

Certainly, nothing was more important for long-term survival than getting married and having babies. So, pioneer clans took seriously their role in serving as matchmaking agencies for their members. While church growth was important for bringing souls to Jesus, it was also important for sustaining pioneer communities. Since the clan had to bring in new blood to avoid excessive inbreeding, clans tended to struggle against each other to attract new members. Converting young women from rival clans and their churches provided one way to bring brides to the brethren. Arguments over doctrine took on graver importance when they might make the difference between finding a wife and living alone. And so, skill in doctrinal argument became a crucial networking skill.

We can see the role of doctrine in frontier survival through an interesting record written by William's dear friend and pastor, the Reverend Samuel Newman. In the church minutes of the Linfield Creek Baptist Church of 1757, he wrote:

> About this time arose certain of the favorers of that Scriptureless Practice, infant sprinkling, and in a disorderly manner, called on Alexander Miller to their assistance, to go ridicule and slander our ministers, and our church officer who at the time did officiate the office of deacon by church's appointment, which said Miller had before aspersed our Rev. Brother of being a Baptist.

Accordingly, on Wednesday the 21st of September, 1757, the said Miller and a rude assembly with him, in a disorderly manner, without leave, or previous notice given to the church, or persons by him accused, opened our meeting house, and assumed our pulpit, and there slanderously, falsely, and contrary to Christian Rule and Order (did) despitefully use our Minister and Brother, the Deacon, with opprobrious speeches, of spite and malice, entirely untruth, and unknown to the said parties; and of which we are fully convinced, neither of them guilty of the errors by him charged, neither in word, thought, or deed, which said irregular and disorderly practice of his, has since occasioned animosities in the neighborhood, and he, the said Miller, hath been thereby instrumental, in the hands of Satan, to disturb the church's peace, and the peace of the neighborhood, this being a time of noted peace with us in the midst of difficulties elsewhere. [144]

It seems that the Rev. Miller mentioned here was one of the "dreaded Presbyterians" of the area. In seeking publicly to confront the "grievous errors" of the Baptists, perhaps he sought either to gain back lost members or gain nubile youths for his own community.

We have no reason to doubt the deep convictions that supported the doctrines of baptism at the heart of the conflict. At the same time, we have a hard time imagining that those convictions justified a committee going over to disrupt another church's services. One might suspect that something more than mere disagreement over the meaning of the Scriptures motivated such deep convictions.

We note the outrageous character of the dispute even more clearly when the Rev. Newman goes on to describe the "difficulties elsewhere." He referred to the fact that the French and Indian War threatened the whole community with extinction, Baptists and Presbyterians alike. The good reverend goes on to describe the dangers:

> The Wednesday following this riotous action, it pleased God to permit the Heathen (Indians) to fall on our settlements and disordered the whole worse than they had done themselves, the week before. A Just retaliation for such unheard of proceedings and measures they had [taken]. The aforesaid proceedings, together with the Indian troubles, Saturday in January 1758: at which time the kind providence of God enabled us to regulate so many of the disorders that attended us, as that which comfort and peace, we could proceed. . . . January 1758 . . . After this time the spring coming on, the Indian troubles continued, and all opportunities of meetings were taken from us; and not only so I but the whole neighborhood forced either to go into forts or over the mountains to escape their rage in the month of June following. [145]

In the middle of a war, with the constant threat of danger from the French and Indians, the believers fought their own doctrinal war, struggling for control of the town. Newman saw the "Indian troubles" as direct proof of God's disapproval of the Presbyterians and their invasion of his church. But he also recognized that the divine retribution shut down both churches altogether.

These troubles eventually led to the decision of the Newmans and Castleberrys to pick up stakes and move on. In 1765, the families moved to Newberry County, South Carolina. There they once again planted a congregation, the Bush River Baptist Church. By 1775, they had moved on to Wilkes County, Georgia, to found the Long Creek Baptist Church. For three generations, the Newman and Castleberry families had intermarried, along with other members of their clan. The records of their church in Georgia depict it as one of the most fractious, hard drinking, infighting congregations you could imagine. [146] Ironically, both Castleberry and Newman members got excommunicated (at various times) for alleged misbehavior.

Despite the unspiritual behavior these frontier churches sometimes displayed, their doctrine remained pure. Let the church without fault cast the first stone, after removing the log from its own eye! New doctrines always entered the group along with specific social needs. Even the most cursory study of the history of theology shows that doctrinal controversies are always both a spiritual and a political matter. Arguments from Scripture always get offered in support of new doctrines, *but the issues always get settled by a vote.* Almost invariably, disgruntled feet exercise a subsequent vote. In any case, church politics always get involved in the resolution of disagreements of all kinds, whether doctrinal or not.

> **CHURCH POLITICS ALWAYS GET INVOLVED IN THE RESOLUTION OF DISAGREEMENTS OF ALL KINDS, WHETHER DOCTRINAL OR NOT.**

The story goes on through the generations until the emergence of William's great grandson, William Castleberry. In the early and mid-1800s, a new doctrinal controversy arose among the Baptists in Georgia, called the Missionary Movement. William, like his ancestors before him, was a Landmark Baptist, believing that the only true Christians were Baptists. His rigid and exclusive doctrinal position earned for him and his coreligionists the nickname, "hard-shell Baptists." Since he believed that only the elect could be saved, he saw no need to send missionaries to the heathen. He had fought against Native Americans and did not believe in evangelizing them.

As a result of his (totally unbiblical) convictions, William struggled hard against the Missionary Baptists. Year after year through the early 1840s, the records of the Georgia Baptist Convention indicate that William gave precisely nothing to missions. [147] One year he gave the sum of 1¢—almost certainly a protest offering. As it became clear that the Missionary Baptists had won the convention, William took his inheritance and moved his family to Alabama.

In Alabama, William networked with likeminded people to found Salem Baptist Church in Coosa County. The church followed the lines of what would come to be known as Primitive Baptist doctrine. There the Castleberrys struggled for survival with their clan throughout the Civil War and Reconstruction. They weren't alone. Believers of like faith supported them in a warm and yet fractious community. The bloodlines of the community demonstrate frequent links in and out of the original Pennsylvania and Virginia settlers who propelled the Baptist movement through the history of the Southeast.

THE ROLE OF DOCTRINE

I find it fascinating to note the role that religious doctrine played in holding together the pioneer clans that settled the American frontier. Baptists networked with Baptists, sometimes splitting into rival Baptist factions. Presbyterians networked with Presbyterians (sometimes splitting into rival factions). Methodists networked with other Methodists (splitting and reuniting and struggling with each other). Yet sometimes people found it to their advantage to leave their group and join a rival denomination. That decision usually involved intermarriage. Doctrinal convictions tended to follow family ties. As Ruth said to Naomi, "Your people will be my people, and your God my God." [148]

An old southern joke (especially as Jerry Clower used to tell it) relates the story of a Baptist boy who wanted to marry a Methodist girl. His father objected, stating that the girl wasn't a Christian.

"Sure she's a Christian," objected the son. "Her folks all attend the Methodist Church devoutly."

The father retorted that she couldn't be a Christian, as she hadn't been properly baptized. "Well, they sprinkled her head real good," said the young man.

"'Tain't no good," insisted the father.

"Well, what if she was to go out in the water with our pastor up to her waist, would that fix it?"

"She might as well stay on the bank."

"Well, what if she went out in the water up to her neck, would that do?"

"No," said the father, "she's got to wet her head."

"That's what I thought," concluded the son. "It's the head that really matters." [149]

It would be funny, if it weren't so ridiculous. At least, that's the way it looks from the twenty-first century. But things looked very different in 1845. It seems a curious thing that doctrine should have been such a source of both cohesion and division in Early America. Today, doctrine seems hardly important at all to many Christians. The idea that one church or denomination has an exclusive hold on the truth, or an exclusive claim to being true Christians, is anathema to most of us. Why did earlier generations focus so heavily on doctrine?

We might explain that the rigidity of doctrinal positions resulted from modernist thinking. In the past two or three centuries, the Age of Reason gave rise to the belief that we could gain absolute certainty through reason. So modernist Christians studied hard to find the exact truth. They exerted great effort to define their positions through tight scriptural reasoning. On such a basis, they attempted to claim the favor of God and superiority over all other views.

But does such an explanation hold true? Did previous generations hold so tightly to their doctrine, merely because of their deep and carefully reasoned convictions based on the Scriptures? Or was something else at stake?

An interesting minute in the records of Salem Baptist Church sheds light on the question. Reverend Edmond T. Akins, my great-great-great grandfather, had recently left the pastorate of the church. Consider one of his biggest problems in ministering there:

April 1855—went into conference and there it was found that no copy of a Bible was in our membership, and that former Pastor (E. T. Akins) rode his mule into Rockford once a week to use a Bible for one hour. A special sacrificial offering was taken which amounted to two dollars, and Elder Steely was authorized to purchase a copy of the Holy Bible, and the Deacons were [named] official Trustees of this copy of the Bible. The Bible is to be used in our Meeting House and in our Grave Yard and not subject to loan to anyone for use in any other place. [150]

Apparently, not many could study the Bible in any great depth to try to find the truth. In Salem, no one even owned a Bible. Some of the church members probably couldn't have read the Bible even if they had obtained access to one. I don't know how widely the Bible may have been available in other regions of the country. I just realize that, whatever reason my Baptist relatives in Salem had for separating themselves from other Christians, it couldn't have been based on their detailed, personal exegesis of the Bible.

On the other hand, people had become adept at memorizing rote facts, like Bible verses, as Mark Twain describes in his nineteenth-century novel *Tom Sawyer*. [151] They knew precisely the doctrine of their church, as it got passed from preacher to preacher and from member to member. But most of them were not profound students of the Bible, great philosophers, or theologians.

So it would appear that the main purpose of doctrine at the time was to maintain the boundaries of the social community. Doctrine helped my Baptist ancestors hold off interlopers who would pick off members for their own kith and kin and thus erode the security of the pioneer clan.

TODAY'S DOCTRINAL SCENE

Things have changed a great deal in America since my ancestors carved out a life on the frontier. The role of doctrine in churches has changed. The dogmatic defense of doctrinal positions used to be essential for the preservation and survival of pioneer clans on the frontier. But American culture has changed, along with the economy and the family. People no longer look to congregations and clans for their primary access to economic opportunity, but rather to educational credentials and professional networks.

While earlier times expected nepotism, today we condemn it. Americans no longer look for spouses exclusively from among their family friends or local communities. They often search for a mate through their larger social networks, or even on the Internet. People used to marry within the confines of their local church or local association of denominational churches. Now people routinely marry believers (or unbelievers) whose doctrinal positions vary from the ones they learned as youths. We often hear the phrase, "doctrine divides, but love unites."

> ❝
> **FINDING THE TRUTH AND MAKING A WHOLE-HEARTED COMMITMENT TO IT IS OF VITAL IMPORTANCE.**
> ❞

At the same time, many people decry the decline of doctrine in the church. I have no question that people today don't think hard enough about the truths of Christianity. Finding the truth and making a whole-hearted commitment to it is of vital importance. But perhaps doctrine has never been as pristine and well-reasoned as many would imagine.

In any case, doctrine no longer serves as the most important boundary marker for Christian communities. In most congregations, we find a bewildering difference of opinion on issues of doctrine and practice among the members. While in my doctoral program, I did some research at my home church to find out what the members believed. Although our denomination puts a great deal of emphasis on our doctrinal statement, it turns out that the members don't concern themselves much about it. The wide diversity of religious views in the church really surprised me.

THE OPEN GATES OF TODAY'S CHURCHES

For the most part, people no longer choose to worship with a particular congregation because they think it has the best doctrine. Instead of seeking to maintain tight boundaries, most churches try to install more gates that will allow people to enter and join their community life, building wider networks to the rest of the Christian community. As a result, people go in and out of those gates at a rate unprecedented in church history.

The decline of doctrine as the primary boundary marker of Christian communities has mirrored a significant decline of denominational loyalty. A recent study by Ellison Research showed that about 70 percent of churchgoers in America would consider attending a church of a different denomination if they had to leave their current church for some reason. [152] The Pew Forum on Religion and Public Life recently found that 44 percent of adults have changed their church affiliation over the course of their lives. [153] Today's Americans would seem much less loyal to denominations than previous generations. (Most Roman Catholics, however, remain staunchly loyal to their church. Some 60 percent say they would not consider attending a different denomination. In contrast, only 16 percent of Protestants say they would never change their denominational identity.) [154]

Why do people change denominations in today's America? Why do they not remain in the churches of their birth? As always, they may change because of intermarriage. But now the change often comes because they have to leave their homes to find new jobs or to attend a university. In the process, they sometimes lose the habit of attending church. As always, some people change churches because of powerful religious experiences that revive their faith. Other people change churches because they don't agree with the teachings of their church and so go searching for a church that believes what they believe. But today, that seems like one of the least likely reasons people change churches.

> **IN TODAY'S WORLD, PEOPLE DON'T GO LOOKING FOR A NEW CHURCH TO SEE WHICH ONE HAS THE PUREST DOCTRINE.**

In today's world, people don't go looking for a new church to see which one has the purest doctrine. Rather, they ask which church will provide them the best experience of God's presence and the best community in which they and their families can live out their faith with other Christians. At work and school and other places, they'll network with Christians who attend other churches, but who hold the same faith in Jesus as they do. They will tolerate subtle and even large differences in doctrine, so long as they feel God's presence and feel loved and accepted and useful in their church.

THE REALITY OF GOD

In my old Alabama family, multiple factors led emerging generations to leave Salem Baptist Church (which now, thoroughly depopulated, no longer holds regular meetings and is preserved along with its storied graveyard as a historic landmark). In the 1920s, my great-grandfather, Joseph Wiley "Jody" Castleberry, found himself homeless when the local banker cheated him out of the new house he had built. He lost everything and had to leave the county to find work. He wound up as a tenant farmer in Marbury, Alabama. Separated from his land, his church, and his ancestors' graves, he became both penniless and depressed. Undoubtedly, his faith suffered in the process.

Everything changed one evening in 1930 when he wandered into the Fire Baptized Holiness Church and experienced a brand new baptism. His ancestors had been arguing with other Christians about baptism for 200 years; but this time, it wasn't an argument about water, but an experience of fire! My great-grandfather believed that his baptism in the Holy Ghost and fire had utterly burned out the sin in his life. He believed that God had entirely sanctified him. The fire of God had overwhelmed his sinful nature . . . and his life changed forever.

Jody had been a popular song leader and had published many gospel hymns. He had served as a leader in his church for decades. But his new experience of the reality of God felt so powerful, he concluded he had never really known God before. He discarded some of his old doctrines in favor of a new experience; but new doctrines immediately came in to take their place. Jody remained a Pentecostal for the rest of his life, ending up in a denomination in which, in due time, my grandfather, my father, and I would all hold ministerial status.

Doctrine is important. Integrity demands that we think through our beliefs carefully and do the absolute best we can to understand the Bible and the truth about God. I believe that we can understand the Bible and that we can find the truth through the use of reason, revelation, tradition, and direct experience. I believe in the authority of the Bible to correct ideas about God that I derive from reason and experience. I believe the doctrinal positions of my denomination. But I also know that there is something wrong in them. I don't know what it is, but I'm certain that no one has comprehended "the truth, the whole truth, and nothing but the truth." (I hope I never have to swear again to tell that kind of truth in court. I can't reach a standard that tall!)

What a dilemma! Something I believe is wrong . . . but I don't know what it is.

We all have blind spots. That's the nature of human knowing. While absolute truths exist, no one knows them absolutely. Who shall deliver us from this dilemma?

Jesus Christ, Himself. He is real, and He makes Himself known to us in real presence. Jesus is the answer to my partial knowledge. I may not know everything, but I know Him. I have encountered Him in person, over and over again. He is the same Jesus that the Bible tells me about, so I believe in it and study it to know more about Him. I think hard about what I believe and seek to integrate it with what I know from reason and science, as well as the Scriptures. I pray and obey and take up His mission and walk with Him, through the ministry of the Holy Spirit. And in the process, I find myself seeking to network with other people who have dedicated themselves to Christ and who walk in obedience to His mission.

I thank God for the Assemblies of God network and the way it has empowered me to obey the mission of Jesus. I plan to serve God loyally in my denomination for the rest of my

> **I FIND MYSELF SEEKING TO NETWORK WITH OTHER PEOPLE WHO HAVE DEDICATED THEMSELVES TO CHRIST AND WHO WALK IN OBEDIENCE TO HIS MISSION.**

life. I thank God for the Baptist networks to which my ancestors belonged, and the Mennonite churches before that, and the Roman Catholic Church before that. I thank God for the Presbyterians— they sharpened the faith of my Baptist forebears by struggling against them. They sharpened my own faith by educating me for five years in one of their seminaries. I love the independent churches that have shaped my family's faith. I love the whole constellation of denominations and fellowships in the kingdom net. They have all had a part in sustaining the faith of our families.

I count it such a privilege to be knotted together with all of them in God's kingdom network. But no part of the church is greater than the whole church, and no network is whole without the Great Networker.

BEYOND THE TRADITIONAL CHURCH

Most people think of a church as a body of believers led by a pastor (whether full or part-time). The members meet on Sundays (or Saturdays, if it is a sabbatarian group) and often on other days of the week. They have a building they traditionally call "the church," confusing themselves and everyone else about what a church really is. They share a doctrinal position and belong to denominations or other forms of interchurch fellowship. They have deacons and Sunday school teachers and . . . well, you know the drill.

Beginning in the late 1940s and speeding up rapidly in the 1970s, the definition of "church" has been changing. Several kinds of organizations began to spring up to ensure that the church's ministry got accomplished in every possible way. Parachurch organizations such as Young Life and Campus Crusade and Intervarsity rose up to attend to the needs of high school and college students. Publishing houses such as NavPress and Thomas Nelson and magazines like *Christianity Today* rose up to assist the church in its teaching ministry to lay people. Radio and television ministries, and (more lately) Internet ministries proliferated as well, offering teaching and other church functions in new ways.

> **NO PART OF THE CHURCH IS GREATER THAN THE WHOLE CHURCH, AND NO NETWORK IS WHOLE WITHOUT THE GREAT NETWORKER.**

Contemporary Christian music was born, moving recorded musical worship into spheres beyond the local church. Ministries such as the

Navigators rose up to attend to the question of discipleship. To assist denominations and churches in training their ministers, interdenominational seminaries sprang up, such as Gordon-Conwell and Fuller Theological seminaries. Ministries such as Prison Fellowship emerged to minister to prisoners. Military chaplaincy grew more important, as well as chaplaincies dedicated to everything from hospitals to sports teams to rodeos to bikers. The list of ministries and their types is endless.

All of these ministries have had the significant effect of unifying Christians across the lines of churches and denominations. But they have unquestionably broken the monopoly of traditional local churches over worship, fellowship, missionizing, and discipleship training.

In my younger years, a book titled *The Problem with Wineskins,* by Howard Snyder, caused a lot of Christians to seriously rethink the "packaging" of the church into "churches." [155] Today, churches are no longer all-purpose, one-stop shopping for all spiritual needs. Christians no longer get all of their teaching or worship or fellowship or even the administration of baptism and the Lord's Supper from a single local church. As a matter of fact, many Christians think of their "real church" as their small group or parachurch ministry.

My friend, Jon Sharpe, serves as Executive Director of a Seattle area ministry called C3 Leaders. Jon, a brilliant networker, has organized dozens of forums in our city that provide effective small-group fellowship for business executives and other key leaders. Together, the members of C3 Leaders see themselves as part of the network God is building to bring the Seattle area into a new awakening to Christ in commerce, culture, and community. The connections we make constantly feed into our work, our families, and our churches. And in a real way, our C3 group is very much one of the "churches" we attend. Parts of our lives are fed there that our full-service congregations cannot feed.

Ministries like C3 Leaders form part of a worldwide movement often referred to as the Faith at Work Movement. [156] Business people across the world have discovered they need specialized ministries that can speak to their particular struggles, challenges, and opportunities in the workplace, the market, and the public square. [157] Centers have been established in the world's top universities—such as Yale and Princeton—to study and even to support this trend. Most local churches don't have enough business owners and executives to offer the kind of support these small groups can provide, and for many business people, their workplace may double as a form of the church.

WHAT IS A CHURCH?

With so many different kinds of ministries doing the work of the church, what makes a group of believers into a church? First, the members' relationship to Jesus makes them part of His body. When they gather, the real presence of Jesus works by the power of the Holy Spirit, energizing their worship or evangelization or fellowship or study. Jesus is preached (or at least confessed) in their midst and named in their prayers. He is perceived in their personal piety and proclaimed to the public. The members love each other because they recognize the presence of Jesus in their brothers and sisters. They joyfully celebrate baptism and the Lord's Supper together.

Having adopted the mission of God as their own, the community of believers work to fulfill the Great Commission in the power of the Holy Spirit. United together, they recognize their kinship with other followers of Jesus. Committed to holiness, they minister to those who fall into sin with patience and kindness. They believe in the whole gospel, and they want to reach the whole world with the good news of the kingdom. God can and will use them to make the world's greatest social network bigger and bigger.

WORKING THE NET

If you're a pastor, you may not be able to complete the following exercises as they stand. Some pastors feel suspicious about other pastors attending their services, in fear that they will steal their members. Exercise good discretion. If pastors want to attend a service at another church, they should take care to establish a trusting relationship with the pastor of that church beforehand. Never attend another pastor's church without calling to ask for permission.

1. Make a list of ten Christians who are your coworkers. You might also choose people you know well because of other associations or contexts. What churches do they attend? Have you ever attended their churches for any special event?

Name of CoWorker	Church Affiliation	Have You Visited?

2. In a spirit of Christian cooperation, arrange with a friend to attend a special event at each of the churches represented among your friends over the course of a year. *Be sure not to neglect your own home church in doing so.* The point of this exercise is not to abandon your home church, but rather to connect with Christians you don't know yet and gain an appreciation of their insights into following Jesus. Ask your friend to introduce you to a few leaders in the church. If you see people at the church you already know, make sure to greet them. After you get home, make a list of everyone you met and connected with. You might send them a Facebook friend request or follow them on Twitter or send them a note on LinkedIn. Both at the event and in the days to follow, remain sensitive to opportunities to serve as the Holy Spirit may prompt you. You may want to send a couple of nice notes to people you met to thank them for making you feel welcome and perhaps to suggest getting together again for coffee or golf or something else.

3. At each church you visit, ask yourself the following questions:

   a. How is this church different from my own? (Not how is it better, but how is it different!)
   b. How is this church similar to my own?
   c. What seems to be most important to this church?
   d. What is the most attractive feature of this church?
   e. What does my friend like the best about this church?

4. Resist the temptation to tell your pastor about how your church needs to change to resemble any of the other ones. If you have a

voice in setting the direction of your church or a ministry within it, you are in a better position to share insights. In that case, go ahead and do so in a mature way that is respectful to those in leadership.

CHAPTER FOURTEEN

IMITATE

MAKING THE CONNECTIONS

I n the previous thirteen chapters, we've looked into the kingdom net that God uses to carry out the primordial mission to save humanity and gather us all together into one people, the bride of Christ. You've worked through some ideas about how the kingdom net functions and how you can offer your own life and work as an instrument for God's use in the mission of God and the Great Commission. You've considered some of the tools you can use to become an effective networker.

But only the Holy Spirit can tell you how to put it all together to fulfill the mission of your life. You'll have to walk out your life in the power and direction of the Spirit if you really want to serve the King and live under His reign.

That's how it works: The kingdom of God can't function among human beings without the Holy Spirit's involvement at the center of it all. If you go back and read the Gospels carefully, especially John 1:19–34 (about John the Baptist and his foretelling of the coming Messiah), you'll see the central role the Holy Spirit plays in the kingdom. John declared three important things about Jesus. He declared (1) that He was the promised Messiah, or "anointed one," who would restore the kingdom of David and the kingdom of God in Israel; (2) that Jesus was not only anointed by the Holy Spirit, but would baptize God's people in the Spirit; (3) that Jesus was the Lamb of God who takes away the sin of the world.

Jesus walked out that threefold mission throughout the Gospels: (1) He modeled the power and anointing of the Spirit, (2) He proclaimed the kingdom of God, and (3) He gave His life as atonement for our sins. Notice the order in which He carried out that mission. He never declared that the kingdom of God was at hand until the Spirit came upon Him at His baptism. After He had made atonement for our sins, He returned to His Father, but not without spending forty more days with His disciples, teaching them about the kingdom and commanding them to wait in Jerusalem until they were baptized with the Holy Spirit. On the Day of Pentecost, the same empowerment that came on Jesus at the time of His baptism also came upon the church, and for the same purpose: to proclaim the kingdom. From that day forward, Christ has reigned over the hearts of men through the Spirit and the Word.

> **YOU CANNOT WORK THE KINGDOM NET WITHOUT THE WORD AND THE SPIRIT IN CHARGE OF YOUR LIFE.**

The Word of God in writing, contained in the Bible, will lay down all the principles of godly character and behavior that we need in order to live righteously. The Holy Spirit within us leads us into all other truth: revealing to us the will of God, renewing our minds, making the Scriptures alive to us, inspiring us with a sense of personal calling and direction. You cannot work the kingdom net without the Word and the Spirit in charge of your life.

What does it look like when God's people fully submit to the Father's reign, weaving and working the kingdom net in the midst of their everyday lives? Let me give you another example.

KENDRA VANDERMEULEN AND THE SEATTLE CHRISTIAN FOUNDATION

Several of my friends in Seattle are not only great kingdom networkers, but they also helped create today's hyper-connected social network. Nobody exemplifies that group better than Kendra VanderMeulen.

Nothing less than a business superwoman, Kendra's career included stints as President of AT&T's Conversant Systems, Senior Vice President and General Manager of the Wireless Data Division of AT&T Wireless, and Executive Vice President (Mobile) at InfoSpace. She currently serves as President of the Seattle Christian Foundation, an affiliate of the National Christian Foundation. She also serves on a number of corporate and nonprofit boards, including B-Square, Inrix, Perlego Systems, and SoulFormation.

When she started college, Kendra never imagined the business career she would go on to achieve. As a young girl in the 1970s, she thought she would become a teacher, so she enrolled at Marietta College as a math major. During her senior year, her father lost his job and she had to find a way to finish her degree in the cheapest way possible. She realized that she could finish her degree fastest by not getting a teaching certificate. That decision set the course for the rest of her life.

As graduation approached, Kendra went to the college placement office and applied for jobs with companies looking for math majors. In 1973, computer science was in its infancy, but AT&T (known as Ma Bell before it split up into several companies in 1984) realized that it would have to increase automation of the telecommunications industry to operate in the future. Not many colleges offered computer science majors at that time, and the whole world didn't have enough programmers to meet AT&T's software needs. So AT&T's Bell Laboratories started hiring math majors (mostly women!) and turning them into programmers. Kendra went to work for them right out of college.

Her boss recognized her as "smarter than the average bear," and AT&T rewarded her talent and hard work by promoting her to the position of engineer and sending her off to Ohio State University for a master's degree in computer science. Faced with the challenge of completing a two-year program in just nine months, Kendra got it done. Up through the ranks she rose. The furious advance of technology and the breakup of AT&T's monopoly on phone service in the United States provided unbelievable opportunities for advancement.

Kendra's work put her at ground zero for the networking revolution that transformed telecommunications. She became a key leader in many of the advances that created such things as cellular phones and wireless Internet devices. As she rose, she moved from the technical development side of the industry to the business side. When AT&T started creating new companies, they named her president of a company called Conversant Systems. "Making the move from development to business, responsible for marketing, sales, manufacturing, and development, gave me an MBA in the School of Hard Knocks," she chuckled when I interviewed her about her career. The company sent her off for short-term training at Sloan, Harvard, and other top business schools along the way, and her skills as a leader increased. Along the way, she married fellow computer scientist William Snider, and the couple had two children.

By 1988, Kendra had become Director of Network Signaling and Databases, deep into the details that would create the infrastructure for the computer and telecommunications networks we know today. In 1991, she became president of the computer systems division of Cincinnati Bell Information Systems—the "cowboy days" of the cellular phone business. Craig McCaw of McCaw Cellular was buying up cellular companies all over the country to build the world's largest cellular network. Kendra could see the future unfolding years ahead of time.

AT&T had a stodgy corporate culture in those days, what Kendra calls a "Forty-Two Long Club." She says, "If you weren't a man who wore a size forty-two long suit, you didn't really belong." Kendra loved the casual, inclusive, visionary environment at McCaw, so she went to work for them as Vice President and General Manager of their Wireless Data Division. In 1996, she launched the first wireless internet devices—what we now call smart phones. Today's totally inter-connected, globally networked world wouldn't exist without what she and her colleagues did in the early 1990s. When AT&T bought McCaw Cellular and turned it into AT&T Wireless, Kendra wound up back at AT&T, where she stayed until 2001.

Kendra's last few years at AT&T took a physical toll on her, as doctors diagnosed her with cancer in 1998. Still, she continued to work as she battled the disease. In 1999, she received the Catherine B. Cleary award as the Outstanding Woman Leader of AT&T, but as she turned fifty in 2001, she announced her retirement. Shortly afterward, the 911 attacks occurred, the tech bubble burst, and she lost half of her net worth. She found herself out of work and out of gas. With no idea where to go or what to do, she felt "scared out of her mind." She needed work and a purpose, because for a very long time she had based her identity on her performance. "What now, Lord? Will I ever matter again in this world?"

Using the people networks she had built over the years in the telecommunications business, she began to consult for several companies and served on several corporate boards. In 2003, she took a job at InfoSpace and sold her stock in 2005 at its peak price. At that point, financially secure, she sensed the Holy Spirit's direction that her business career had ended. She said to the Lord, "I sure hope you have something in mind. I'm too young to quit being productive." Shortly afterward, she got a call from our mutual friend, Ed McCahill. Ed is a man full of the Holy Spirit and wisdom. He said to her, "There's this little thing starting up downtown called the Seattle Christian Foundation. They've asked me to lead it, but every time I pray about it, I see your face. I think you should call them." "Great," she replied. "I'll do that."

Kendra didn't know anyone on the board of the new organization. She didn't know what the foundation was supposed to do. After interviewing, she had the attitude, "This is interesting, but what does it have to do with me?" Nevertheless, she agreed to join the Advisory Board of the foundation. Two or three weeks later, fellow board member Andy Toles, a wonderful attorney from Skip Li's firm who also walks in the Spirit, asked her to attend the Generous Giving Conference sponsored by the National Christian Foundation (NCF) in Atlanta. She agreed to go.

The conference totally transformed her concept of giving. She and her husband had always been generous givers, but the conference became a spiritual turning point for her. While before she had given generously from her surplus, she now realized that *all* her money belonged to God. She was only God's money manager. The question had been, "How much can we give?" Now, it became, "How much can we keep?"

When she returned home to Seattle and shared her new spiritual insight, her husband agreed that their wealth really belonged to God. They tripled their giving! Accustomed to writing five-figure checks, they began to write six-figure checks to support the kingdom causes they felt passionate about. They also experienced a new level of joy in giving. Her new experiences of generosity helped to shape the Seattle Christian Foundation as well, and in 2007, she accepted the position of president.

While Kendra's business career helped create a whole new dimension in computer and telecommunications networking, her career in philanthropy has focused on the kingdom net. She brings her solid people skills and amazing technical skills together to work with others God has entrusted with His money, to help them see the true nature of biblical stewardship and how they can maximize their management of it. The funny thing is, she doesn't see herself as a master networker. She just uses her skills to connect people with organizations that serve the causes for which God has given them a passion.

"My job is to mobilize an unprecedented abundance of kingdom resources to accomplish every good work," she says. That's the vision statement of the National Christian Foundation; but it's also her personal vision. "I serve givers and help them along their journey of generosity, which includes spiritual and technical issues," she explains. "It's just technical enough to keep the computer scientist in me interested."

Kendra doesn't see herself as good at a lot of skills that people normally associate with networking. But the proof is in the pudding. She follows the Holy Spirit's lead in weaving connections between people to facilitate the advance of the kingdom all around the world. She helps people navigate the financial technicalities that make it possible to maximize their use of God's resources. She walks them through their fears, an especially important task in today's turbulent economy. With the help of the Holy Spirit, she ignites and tends their fires until they can put them in the right fireplaces. As a result, last year alone the Seattle Christian Foundation managed to channel significant funding into more than 500 organizations. Beneficiaries included tiny ministries and large operations, global causes and local ones, community development agencies like World Vision, Christian universities like Seattle Pacific and Northwest University, Christian schools, orphanages, rescue missions, and other kingdom priorities. The skills she learned as a manager and leader at AT&T and other companies

> **THE GROWTH OF THE KINGDOM IS THE GROWTH OF GOD'S PEOPLE NET.**

are now deployed in the world's greatest network, and she's sending a message to the world like never before.

THE NATURE OF KINGDOM NETWORKING

So what is the nature of kingdom networking? Jesus makes it clear in several of His parables that the kingdom of God is advancing forcefully. [158] It is the nature of the kingdom to expand. In one parable, He compares it to a mustard seed that starts off as the smallest of seeds and grows until it becomes a spreading tree. [159] In another, He likens it to yeast that spreads through a whole lump of dough. [160] In still another, He compares it to a sower who casts seed onto good ground, yielding thirty, sixty or a hundred times as many seeds. [161] The kingdom is about growth. It's about people. The growth of the kingdom is the growth of God's people net.

Imagine the weaving of a net. One string is tied into a knot when it meets a new string. Each string goes on and connects to other strings and ties new knots. Pretty soon, many strings get connected to each other and, through the net, all the strings get connected, whether directly or indirectly. That's the way God's people network.

> **JESUS TIES EVERY ONE OF HIS FOLLOWERS IN THE WORLD TO EVERY OTHER ONE THROUGH THE KINGDOM NET.**

Jesus ties every one of His followers in the world to every other one through the kingdom net, and the net grows bigger and bigger, and more and more exciting, as we weave our personal networks broader into the world and deeper into the church. The more people you know, the more people you can introduce to Jesus. The more Christians you know, the more you can work with others to bring people to Jesus. When we work together with other Christians, we maximize our fulfillment of the mission.

I love the work of the people I've briefly profiled in this book—Jesse Owens, Skip Li, Kendra VanderMeulen, Rob Smith, Jeff Rogers, Jon Sharpe, and others. They all understand how the kingdom net spreads all the way around the world. You may think of your work as purely local. You may imagine it doesn't affect people in other parts of the world. But a little thinking about the people you serve and the products you use or sell will quickly correct that error. As the final haul of God's kingdom net draws nearer and nearer, we see that we live in an ever more globalized world.

> **"**
> **IF YOU BUILD THE NETWORK, THEN THE HOLY SPIRIT WILL COME AND USE IT.**
> **"**

Open your eyes and look! You can expand your network, and your impact for God's kingdom in the world can grow wider.

There has never been a moment greater than the present.

Decide *now* that you will spread your spherical net of influence as far as the kingdom net reaches. Sometimes your networking will apply to an immediate purpose. Sometimes you'll make a sale, connecting people with goods and services they need. Sometimes you'll find help for what you do for God and the world, and other times you'll have the pleasure of serving someone else. Sometimes you'll be able to connect other people in ways that empower their service and their lives. Often you'll see no visible fruit from the life of openness and connectedness that you have cultivated.

Always remember that the kingdom net is not linear, it's spherical. At the subatomic level, substances contain more empty space than particles, and yet they nevertheless appear solid at the visible level. In a similar way, the inner connections of the kingdom may not always seem apparent. Quantum physics has revealed that what happens deep on the inside of reality appears neither logical nor predictable. So it is with the kingdom net. It's such a complex system that you can't trace out causes and effects, but you *can* trust God. As Jesus said, "The wind blows wherever it pleases. You hear its sound, but you cannot tell where it comes from or where it is going. So it is with everyone born of the Spirit." [162]

Ecclesiastes 11:1 says, "Ship your grain across the sea; after many days you may receive a return." In other words, "What goes around, comes around." Kingdom networking depends on people doing things that don't necessarily look logical, obviously purposeful, or immediately useful. But building relationships that God can use creates a circuit through which God's power can run.

Make a decision to "ship your grain across the sea." If you build the network, then the Holy Spirit will come and use it. God's kingdom doesn't build bridges to nowhere. If you build a bridge to someone, two-way traffic will appear. Decide that you will spread the love of God as broadly as you can cast your net. And every day, let the Holy Spirit show you where to cast that net. Not only will you network like Jesus, but He will show up in every connection you make.

WORKING THE NET

1. Remember the list you made in Chapter Two about the ten important people missing from your circle? If you didn't meet with them in the course of the exercises you've already completed, then the time has come. If you can confidently call and set up an appointment to meet with them, do so. If you need a friend to make an introduction, ask them to do it. You have no excuse for not meeting the people most important to your success and the success of God's kingdom. When you meet them, focus on finding out how you can serve them instead of asking them to help you.

2. Now, write a note to the friend who recommended this book. Maybe you could help me with my networking by recommending it to your friends, too. Follow me on Twitter (www.twitter.com/DrCastleberry) or like my Facebook page at www.facebook.com/joseph.castleberry. Check out my blog at www.josephcastleberry.com to see what I've learned about networking since I sent this book off to the publisher. Above all, send me a note at joe@josephcastleberry.com to let me know if this book made an impact on your life or to teach me what you're learning about kingdom networking.

EPILOGUE

"I have seen the future," says an old Woody Allen character, "and it is very much like the present, only longer."

The todays determine the tomorrows, to be sure. But Woody Allen is wrong about the continuity between the past and the present. The tomorrows are increasingly different from the todays and yesterdays. Indeed, the world is on a Titanic-like tryst with an iceberg of time and technology unlike the world has ever seen.

Set the alarm or not, morning comes. Ready or not, the future shows up. Do we show up to the future, pilloried by the past, fearful of the future? Do we back into the future clinging to the past with nostalgia and dread? Or do we face into the future with imagination and hope?

When our dreams no longer tow the future, passing the rope to our fears and small-mindedness, nightmares lurk ahead. Aspirations fertilize actions. Without dreams to seed our stories and mulch our activities, reality is deprived and debased. Without faith in God's reign over tomorrow, the field of dreams would succumb to the weeds of dread.

The Kingdom Net has shown us why we need not despair and how we can dream again, take heart, and gird up our loins. The juggernaut of history has been broken by Jesus and His message of the kingdom. Joseph Castleberry has shown us how we can cast our lot more with divine wisdom and care than with human cleverness.

The constitution of the kingdom, where the protocols of the Prince of Peace supersede the values of Babel and Babylon, bears privileges but also responsibilities. In *The Kingdom Net,* we have seen how the kingdom has already begun, how it can develop and expand through a common covenant among God's people and, most importantly, how our networking can weave the relational structures for a new Great Awakening of the Spirit that the church never thought possible.

Leonard Sweet

AUTHOR OF *VIRAL: HOW SOCIAL NETWORKING IS POISED TO IGNITE REVIVAL*
PROFESSOR AT DREW UNIVERSITY
AND GEORGE FOX UNIVERSITY

NOTES

INTRODUCTION

1. http://www.pewforum.org/christian/global-christianity-exec.aspx
2. http://www.psychologytoday.com/blog/thrive/201205/are-extroverts-happier-introverts

CHAPTER ONE: THE PARABLE OF THE KINGDOM NET

3. Mark 1:17.
4. John 14:12.
5. Romans 10:9.
6. Deuteronomy 17:15.
7. Luke 7:22.
8. Matthew 6:9–13.

CHAPTER TWO: JESUS AND THE KINGDOM NET

9. I'm not attempting formal exegesis of the book of Luke here. Rather, I'm using Luke's telling of Jesus' life to make observations about networking that Luke himself may have had no intention of communicating. My intention is not authoritative exegesis, but rather practical wisdom about networking that Jesus' life illustrates.
10. Romans 8:9–11.
11. Elmer Gray, "Shepherd," in *Holman Illustrated Bible Dictionary*, ed. Chad Brand, Charles Draper, Archie England (Nashville, TN: Holman Bible Publishers, 2003), 1,484.
12. James Charlesworth, class lectures for "Exegesis of the Apocalypse," Princeton Theological Seminary, Fall 1985.
13. Luke 2:43–50.

14. Chris Columbus, *Home Alone.* Twentieth Century Fox Film Corporation (1990).

15. Luke 2:47.

16. Luke 4:22.

17. Luke 4:18–21.

18. There is some degree of uncertainty as to whether Jesus' being allowed to read the scroll in the synagogue liturgy was any sign of His being highly regarded by His fellow worshippers, as any adult may have been eligible to read, including slaves. For a discussion of the practice of reading the Scriptures in first-century Palestine, see Michael Graves, "The Public Reading of Scripture in Early Judaism." *(Journal of the Evangelical Theological Society* 50/3; Louisville, KY: Evangelical Theological Society, September 2007), 467–87.

19. Luke 4:24.

20. Acts 4:13.

21. A. C. Myers, *The Eerdmans Bible Dictionary* (Grand Rapids, MI.: Eerdmans, 1987), 55.

22. John 1:35–40.

23. www.ted.com/talks/derek_sivers_how_to_start_a_ movement.html

24. John C. Maxwell, *Twenty-One Indispensable Qualities of a Leader* (Nashville: Thomas Nelson, 2000), 5.

25. John 6:9.

26. John 12:20–22. See Myers, 55.

27. Luke 9:54.

28. Mark 10:35–45; cf. Matthew 20:20–28.

29. Acts 12:2.

30. Scholars argue whether John wrote all these books, but I'm convinced that he did.

31. 1 John 4:7–8.

32. Luke 19:10.

33. R. V. G. Tasker, "Matthew" in *New Bible Dictionary,* ed. I. Howard Marshall, A. R. Millard, J. I. Packer, D. J. Wiseman, 3rd ed. (Downers Grove, Ill.: InterVarsity Press, 1996), 739.

34. A. C. Myers, *The Eerdmans Bible Dictionary* (Grand Rapids, MI.: Eerdmans, 1987, 826.

35. John 1:47.

36. John 1:48.

37. John 1:49.

38. R. E. Nixon, "Thomas," in *New Bible Dictionary*, ed. I. Howard Marshall, A. R. Millard, J. I. Packer, D. J. Wiseman, 3rd ed (Downers Grove, Ill.: InterVarsity Press, 1996), 1182–1183.

39. 2 Samuel 12:23.

40. John 20:28.

41. Matthew 10:3; Mark 3:18; Luke 6:14.

42. Genesis 12:3.

43. Luke 4:33–35.

44. Matthew 6:9–13, emphasis added.

CHAPTER THREE: MEETING PEOPLE

45. C. S. Lewis, *The Four Loves,* (New York: Harcourt Books, 1960), 66.

46. Hanna Rosin, "The End of Men." *The Atlantic* 2 (2010). http://www.theatlantic.com/magazine/archive/2010/07/the-end-of-men/308135/2/

47. http://en.wikipedia.org/wiki/Billy_Graham.

48. The Iowa Supreme Court recently ruled that an employer in that state can fire an employee because of sexual attraction. While such behavior may be legal in some places, it is unfortunate at best. See http://www.cnn.com/2012/12/21/justice/iowa-irresistible-worker/index.html

49. Ronald H. Martin, ed., *Terence: Adelphoe* (Cambridge, UK: Cambridge University Press, 1976), 13.

50. Miguel de Unamuno, *Del Sentimiento Trágico de la Vida: La Agonía del Cristianismo.* http://es.wikisource.org/wiki/Del_sentimiento_trágico_de_la_vida:_I.

51. If you're in East Asia in a business or diplomatic setting, and it's your turn to meet someone, you'll want to present your card with two hands and a slight bow as your first action, taking the other person's card in turn. You must then take special care to read the card silently in front of them, showing that you

have taken it seriously. If you're in such a formal situation, ask an experienced person to teach you the card etiquette. You'll avoid the embarrassment I caused myself at a particular consulate that shall go unnamed.

52. L. M. Montgomery, *Anne of Green Gables*, 1908. http://www.gutenberg.org/ebooks/45

53. Francis Ford Coppola, *The Godfather: Part II*. Paramount Pictures Corporation, 1974.

54. Malcolm Gladwell, *The Tipping Point: How Little Things Make a Big Difference*. (NewYork: Little, Brown and Company, 2000), 177–181, 185–186. NPR "Staff, Don't Believe Facebook: You Only Have 150 Friends." *NPR*. June 4, 2011. http://www.npr.org/2011/06/04/136723316/dont-believe-facebook-you-only-have-150-friends).

CHAPTER FOUR: THE MISSION OF GOD AND THE HUMAN MISSION

55. Chi-Dooh Li, *Buy This Land* (Seattle: Create Space Independent Publishing Platform, 2012), 93.

56. Genesis 1:27.

57. Genesis 1:28.

58. To look at the original text of Beowulf, go to http://www.fordham.edu/halsall/basis/beowulf-oe.asp

59. Genesis 1:28.

60. Nancy Pearcey, *Total Truth: Liberating Christianity from Its Cultural Captivity* (Wheaton, IL: Crossway, 2008), 47.

CHAPTER FIVE: JESUS THE NETWORKER

61. Ephesians 2:20.

62. Luke 5:8.

63. Luke 5:10.

64. Luke 18:28–30.

65. Luke 5:12–15.

66. Luke 14:12–14.
67. I've written more about this parable in *Your Deepest Dream: Discovering God's True Vision for Your Life* (Colorado Springs: NavPress, 2012).
68. Luke 16:8–9.
69. Luke 6:20–22.
70. Ecclesiastes 9:11–12.
71. Proverbs 10:18.
72. Luke 5:14–16.
73. Luke 5:18–19.
74. Luke 5:25–26.

CHAPTER SIX: NETWORK MAINTENANCE

75. Mark 8:1–8.
76. John 6:1–14.
77. John 6:35.
78. The Last Supper is one of the most important events in Jesus's ministry, recorded in all four Gospels. Matthew 26:17–29; Mark 14:12–25; Luke 22:7–38; John 13:1ff.

CHAPTER SEVEN: THE GREAT COMMISSION

79. Ephesians 4:11.
80. Zion Bible Institute is now known as North Point Bible College and is now located in Haverhill, Massachusetts.
81. For the thrilling story of David Wilkerson's ministry in New York City, see David Wilkerson, *The Cross and the Switchblade* (New York: Pyramid Publications, Inc., 1964). An estimated 50 million people in over 30 languages in 150 countries have seen the Hollywood motion picture starring Pat Boone and Erik Estrada. See Don Murray, *The Cross and the Switchblade*. Gateway Productions (1970).
82. See www.globaltc.org and http://global-renewal.org/main/index.php.

83. John 14:30.

84. Genesis 3:15.

85. Genesis 9:11.

86. Genesis 12:3.

87. Isaiah 9:6.

88. Isaiah 7:14.

89. Matthew 3:3.

90. Matthew 3:11; Mark 1:8; Luke 3:16; John 1:31–33.

91. Acts 1:4–8.

92. Matthew 28:18.

93. Matthew 28:19–20.

94. Note carefully that I'm not suggesting the church should take charge of the society, but rather that it should facilitate Christ's rule over the lives of disciples.

95. This account of the fundamentalist-modernist controversy is much too brief, and the topic deserves additional study. It was a fascinating episode in American church history that continues to divide the society. For an excellent study, see George M. Marsden, *Fundamentalism and American Culture* (New York: Oxford University Press, 2006).

96. Matthew 11:5.

97. Katherine Lee Bates, "America the Beautiful," 1895.

98. See John Winthrop's famous speech at https://www.mtholyoke.edu/acad/intrel/winthrop.htmsource.

99. Revelation 11:15.

CHAPTER EIGHT: PAUL THE NETWORKER

100. Acts 21:39; 22:3.

101. Acts 22:3.

102. Galatians 1:14.

103. Acts 8:1–3.

104. Acts 9:11.

105. Acts 4:36–37.

106. Acts 13:1.

107. Stanley Milgram, "The Small World Problem," *Psychology Today,* 1967, Vol. 2, 60–67.

108. Acts 18:2.

109. Acts 18:1–3.

110. Romans 1:10–13.

111. Romans 15:24.

112. Arthur Bloch, *Murphy's Law Book Two: More Reasons Why Things Go Wrong* (New York: Price Stern Sloan, 1980), 47.

113. C. E. B. Cranfield, *A Critical and Exegetical Commentary on the Epistle to the Romans,* vol II. (Edinburgh: T. & T. Clark, 1979), 791–792. Ernst Käsemann disagrees, pontificating that "Herodion . . . in spite of his name . . . does not have anything to do with the Herodians. That is also true of Aristobulus in v. 10, of whom one must even doubt whether he is a Christian." Though Käsemann was a scholar of significant note, he totally misses the point in this case and offers no case for his view. Cranfield's position is clearly stronger. See Ernst Käsemann, *Commentary on Romans* (Grand Rapids, MI: Eerdmans), 414. In the end, it doesn't matter whether Aristobulus was "the" Aristobulus, but rather that he was wealthy and prominent and had a household to be reckoned with.

114. Cranfield, 792.

115. Cranfield, 792.

116. Mark 15:21.

117. Acts 17:6–7.

118. Cranfield, 806.

119. For more discussion of this question, see F. F. Bruce, *Romans, The Tyndale New Testament Commentaries* (Grand Rapids, MI: Eerdmans), 280–281. See also J. J. Megitt, "The Social Status of Erasmus (Rom. 16:23)" in *Nestle-Aland Novum Testamentum Graece,* vol. 38, (Deutsche Bibelgesellschaft, 1998), fasc. 3.

120. For those who were not fans of the old television series, *Gilligan's Island,* Thurston Howell the Third was the gazillionaire who was stranded on the island along with his wife and five others castaways.

121. 1 Corinthians 11:1.

CHAPTER NINE: NAME-DROPPING DOS AND DON'TS

122. James Frawley, Jim Henson, Jerry Juhl, Jack Burns, Isidore Mankofsky, Paul Williams, Kenny Ascher, Charles Durning, and Austin Pendleton. *The Muppet Movie.* CBS/Fox Video, 1993.

123. Philippians 2:3–7.

124. Robert Zemeckis, *Forrest Gump.* Paramount Pictures (1994).

CHAPTER TEN: THE WORK NET

125. James 1:27.

126. Howard E Gardner, *Frames of Mind: The Theory of Multiple Intelligences* (New York: Basic Books, 1983, 2011).

127. Joseph had Pharaoh do this in Egypt in Genesis 47:14–21 and his own people were eventually reduced to slavery.

CHAPTER ELEVEN: WRITING NOTES

128. Charles Russell, *Lewis and Clark on the Lower Columbia* 1905, Amon Carter Museum of American Art, Fort Worth, Texas (http://www.cartermuseum.org/artworks/339).

129. 1 Corinthians 12:8.

130. Zemeckis.

CHAPTER TWELVE: WHAT IS THE CHURCH?

131. For an excellent summary of virtually everything that has ever been said about the church by Christian theologians, see Veli-Matti Kärkkäinen, *An*

Introduction to Ecclesiology: Ecumenical, Historical and Global Perspectives (Downers Grove, IL: Intervarsity Press Academic, 2002).

132. 1 Corinthians 11:29.

133. Those who are well read in the semantics of biblical language (viz. James Barr) should recognize that I understand that *katagoreo* and "categorize" do not indeed have the same meaning. But categorizing can be a form of accusation.

134. http://www.christianitytoday.com/ct/2011/january/14.10.html.

135. Ephesians 4:13.

136. Jean-Paul Sartre, *No Exit and Three Other Plays* (New York: Vintage Books, 1949), 47.

137. H. Emil Brunner, *The Word and the World* (London: SCM Press, 1931) 108.

138. C. S. Lewis, *The Last Battle* (New York: Harper Collins, 200), 206.

139. Russell D. Moore, "Where Have All the Presbyterians Gone: Nondenominational churches are the fastest growing in the country." *Wall Street Journal,* February 4, 2011. http://online.wsj.com/article/SB1000142405 2748703437304576120690548462776.html.

140. Hartford Institute for Religion Research. http://hirr.hartsem.edu/research fastfacts/fast_facts.html#sizecong.

CHAPTER THIRTEEN: THE CHURCH AND CHANGE

141. Matthew 11:12.

142. The Pew Forum on Religion and Public Life, Global Christianity: A Report on the Size and Distribution of the World's Christian Population. http://www.pewforum.org/christian/global-christianity-exec.aspx.

143. According to the earliest histories of the Baptist churches of America, William was the first Mennonite to be rebaptized as a Baptist in the history of the country. See Michael J. Puglisi, *Diversity & Accommodation: Essays on the Cultural Composition of the Virginia Frontier* (Knoxville, TN: University of Tennessee Press, 1997), 93; see also Robert B. Semple, *A History of the Rise and Progress of the Baptists in Virginia* (Richmond, 1810); David Benedict, *A*

General History of the Baptist Denomination in America, and Other Parts of the World, 2 vols. (Boston, 1813).

144. John Houston Harrison. *Settlers by the Long Grey Trail: Some Pioneers to Old Augusta County, Virginia, and Their Descendants of the Family of Harrison and Allied Lines.* (Clearfield Company, 1935), 178–9.

145. Ibid.

146. *Minutes of the Long Creek Baptist Church, Warren County, Georgia in Four Volumes,* Vol. I, 1786–1883. http://users.waymark.net/shmartonak/gawalng.htm.

147. Personal correspondence from Jesse W. Castleberry, MD.

148. Ruth 1:16.

149. Jerry Clower, "Deep Water Baptist," *Classic Clower Power,* MCA Records, Nashville, 2006.

150. *The Central Baptist Association, 150 Years of Ministry,* 1845–1996. A transcription of this record is in my possession.

151. Mark Twain, *The Adventures of Tom Sawyer* (Mineola, NY: Dover, 1998), 18ff.

152. http://www.christianpost.com/news/most-protestant-churchgoers-open-to-other-denominations-36402.

153. http://religions.pewforum.org/reports.

154. http://www.christianpost.com/news/most-protestant-churchgoers-open-to-other-denominations-36402.

155. Howard Snyder, *The Problem of Wineskins: Church Structure in a Technological Age* (Downers Grove, IL: InterVarsity Press, 1975).

156. For a definitive description of the Faith at Work Movement, see David W. Miller, *God at Work: The History and Promise of the Faith at Work Movement* (New York: Oxford University Press, 2007).

157. http://www.nbcnews.com/id/7201269/#.UU5XU781blI.

CHAPTER FOURTEEN: MAKING THE CONNECTIONS

158. Matthew 11:12.

159. Matthew 13:31–32.

160. Matthew 13:33.

161. Matthew 13:1–23.
162. John 3:8.

ABOUT THE AUTHOR

Joseph Castleberry is President of Northwest University in Kirkland, Washington. Raised in Alabama and educated at Evangel University (BA), Princeton Theological Seminary (MDiv), and Columbia University (EdD), he has been a kingdom networker his whole life long, taking his first professional position in ministry in 1983 in Princeton, New Jersey at Nassau Christian Center. He has served as a youth pastor, campus minister, church planter, university professor, missionary to Latin America, community development entrepreneur, seminary dean, and college president. He is also the author of *Your Deepest Dream: Discovering God's True Vision for Your Life* (NavPress, 2012). Dr. Castleberry blogs at www.josephcastleberry.com and you can contact him at joe@josephcastleberry.com. Please like his page at www.facebook.com/joseph.castleberry and follow him on Twitter (www.twitter.com/DrCastleberry).